Clara Moyse Tadlock

Solomon Grinder's Christmas Eve and Other Poems

Clara Moyse Tadlock

Solomon Grinder's Christmas Eve and Other Poems

ISBN/EAN: 9783337317737

Printed in Europe, USA, Canada, Australia, Japan

Cover: Foto ©Thomas Meinert / pixelio.de

More available books at **www.hansebooks.com**

SOLOMON GRINDER'S

CHRISTMAS EVE

AND OTHER POEMS.

CLARA MOCK.

COPYRIGHT, 1885, BY
MRS. CLARA M. TADLOCK.

TO MRS. HORACE MAYNARD,

In Loving Remembrance.

CONTENTS.

SOLOMON GRINDER'S CHRISTMAS EVE	7
MY CONSCIENCE AND I	62
SONG OF THE ZEPHYR	65
PURIFIED	67
LEAVING THE FARM	69
LEAD ME	73
A GARDEN	75
TRANSITION	77
DRIFTING	79
REST	82
CHANGE	84
THE BEAUTIFUL SOUL	91
THE MAGDALEN	94
IN MEMORIAM	98
LAKE CHAUTAUQUA	100
NIGHT	102
IN THE TWILIGHT	104

MOVED TO TOWN	106
ONLY A GLASS	110
NORA	113
PAT DOYLE	120
LIFE'S CHANGEFUL DAY	122
AT THE GATES	134
EPAMINONDAS	141
MY BROTHER'S GRAVE	158
THE SHEPHERD	160
MOTHERLESS	161
NO LIGHT WITHOUT A SHADOW	163
MARA	165
LEAVES FROM A LIFE	167
NAN	193

Solomon Grinder's Christmas Eve.

An old house stood on a quiet street
Round which the surges of travel beat
Yet entered not in. Neglected quite
It seemed, and shrinking away from sight
Behind some oak trees rugged and bare,
And vines that sighed in the chilly air,
And swung their arms to keep themselves
    warm,
Or shake off the snow of the winter's storm.
Smilingly, shyly, the moon peeped forth,
But the wind came whistling down from the
    North;
So, shiv'ring, she wrapped herself again
In her mantle of cloud. Boreas then
Laughingly passed by a window-frame
And rattled the shutters. But the same

Darkness and quietude seemed to say
That life and joy had long passed away.

The home of the miser! what more drear?
Growing more dingy from year to year,
Massive, and frowningly dark it stood,
Wrapped in its garment of solitude,
With an air profound, as of mystery
That hid a tragical history.
Terrible stories of ghostly kind,
Thrilling with dread the childish mind,
By idle people were grimly told.
Others enlarged on the piles of gold
Hidden away in its cellars vast,
Perchance to be spoil of robbers at last!
And children, shuddering, crept away,
Chanced they to pass at the close of day.

An old man looked out into the night
Which quickly followed the short twilight
Of the winter's day, and shook his head
Seeing the last faint light had fled,

But laughed a little, and came outside
To close the shutters.
                    " Providence guide
To their homes in safety wand'rin' feet
That 'll else be lost in this snow and sleet,—
That bothersome shutter! there — it's broke!
Half o' the hinges kin only croak
And groan.— There now, you're up in your place."

The snow came pelting into his face,
But he brushed it away, and walked around
To another door.
                    " Well, I guess I've found
As everythin's as safe as kin be,
I'll see if the Master's a needin' me.
How different — oh, no words kin tell!
If he'd forgive his dear little Nell.—
His *little* Nell! — she's babes of her own,
And finds it hard to struggle alone.—
I can't help much.— Well, there's no use
To worry oneself. There's no excuse
For one God blesses as much as I
To fear he'll forget or pass 'em by —

Them far more worthy! — Stephen, for shame!
For want of faith you're really to blame."
So muttered the old man, shaking the snow
From his clothes, and bringing a pleasant glow
All over his face.

     He closed the door,
Replacing the mat that lay before,
And softly tip-toed into a room
But half relieved from darkness and gloom
By a moderate fire of coal and wood.
Lingering, on the threshold he stood —
For the inmate muttered in undertone,
Supposing himself to be quite alone.

Solomon Grinder, in lonely state,
Sat and looked at the crumbs on his plate;
Then gathered the fragments one by one,
With pointed finger and crooked thumb,
And high in a cupboard placed them away
To be used as food the following day.
"There's no use wasting! money and bread
Are the self-same thing," he slowly said.

"Ah! that you, Stephen? no lamp to-night,
The fire gives out a plenty of light —
No! — no more coal — there! there! that'll do,
I shall have no further need of you
To-night, — so get you away to bed —
Why! what's got into your simple head?"

Old Stephen sighed, and ling'ring still
Said, "Master — I never have done you ill.—
I've waited upon you sick or well —
Thought it no trouble, truth to tell"—

"Ho! ho! you're wanting some extra pay,"
Grumbled the miser.

"Nay! sir, nay!"
Stephen exclaimed, and grew very red,
Looking perplexed as he scratched his head,
And over his forehead drew the hair —
Scarce half covering the wrinkles there,
As his upward brows to meet it went.
His wandering look grew more intent,
Tho' the pale-blue eyes had a far-off look,
And the gentle voice of the old man shook.

"Since with fever you like to ha' died
I've never willin'ly left your side,—
Neither a pleasur'in' 'mongst my kin,
Nor follerin' on where the crowd has been.
And that's a many a year agone—
Full twenty-and-three this Christmas morn
If it's a day. You hed wakened late
Weak as a baby; only the weight
O' the kivers tired ye,"— he smiled and sighed,—
"I'd sooner been the one to ha' died."

"Bosh!" said Solomon, turning aside,
(Could it have been he'd a tear to hide?)
"Look here, old Stephen, you've been as true
As steel to me; but a word or two!
You're weak! poor fellow, awfully weak!
Why don't you go and your fortune seek?
Service is costly! I can't afford—
I really can't! to give you your board.
My simple wants I can well attend,
So fare you better my good old friend.

To give you nothing — it hurts my pride!"

Stephen advanced to his master's side,
And with quiv'ring lip, and moistened eye,
A forced half-laugh, and a heart-felt sigh,
Stood silent a moment.
—"Truth to tell
I was hopin' fer somethin' fer Mistress Nell."

Solomon frowningly looked around,
Gave a disgusted, snarling sound.
"Go to her yourself — no doubt *she* can pay."

Stephen awkwardly sidled away.
"I'll never leave *you*, sir — say no more —
I don't want anything." Opened the door
And, softly closing it, upward went,
The bare stairs sounding his slow ascent.

"Well! well!" said Solomon, "who'd ha' thought
The poor old fellow so overwrought!"
Forgetting himself he poked the fire,
And watched the flames ascending higher,

Adding another shovel of coal —
As 'twere to thaw out his frozen soul.

Near the empty cupboard had its stand
An ancient clock, that with dark long-hand
Pointed, and measured the passing time,
While pendulum ticked an endless rhyme —

> "Time is going —
> Pay what's owing!"

So said Solomon, who should know,
For many a one who debt did owe
Called on him to plead for a short reprieve,
Ere sick or old must a tenement leave;
Always his answer growling came,
After a sentence of useless blame,
"Pay what you owe! we'll be better friends.
You'll all impose on the man who lends.
And as for *your people!* why should I care?
Pay up! or find you a home elsewhere."

Looking down from an opposite space
Was a fair and beautiful pictured face,

With loving eyes of the softest blue,
And cheeks which rivaled the roses hue;
While nut-brown curls o'er the forehead strayed,
And dimples, and smiles round her red lips
    played.
So fair the picture, and full of grace,
It seemed most curiously out of place.
It shone — the one bright spot in the room —
Smiling out on the general gloom.
Always the same through the passing years —
Smiling at merriment, wrongs or tears;
Sometimes to join the general glee,
At others, seem like a mockery!
Always the same, though the scene would
    change,
And some who appeared were actors strange —
This one surely the queerest of all,—
Old and wrinkled, and shriveled, and small;
With eyes that watched ev'ry penny in,
And lips, once pleasant, now parched and
    thin;
With long nose sharpened down to a point,
And limbs which almost seemed out of joint;

And clothes, like the carpet, old and worn,
With curious patches where they'd been torn.

"I wonder what stocks are up," mused he,
"I'm 'fraid to invest in 'Fifty and three'—
If t'others gets in the Bonds 'll go down,
And never a one could be sold in town—
So *they* won't do!—How money does go!
Insurance heavy, and rents come slow—
Too slow! I declare those Smiths must leave
To-morrow! I'd not his oath believe—
Provided he'd set his mind to stay—
Sick or well, they'll get out of *my* way."
Solomon's head on the table leant,
His closing eyes on the coals were bent.—
To Dreamland straight he drifted away.

"Come in!" he lifted his voice to say,
As a loud rap sounded on the door
(The bell had fallen long years before);
But he felt a kind of creeping chill
As the door swung open with a will,

And a stranger entered, booted and spurred,
And seated himself, with never a word.
As closed the door — though no hand was near —
Solomon's hair stood erect with fear!
He felt he *must* speak at any cost,
But his voice was gone, so the breath was lost.
He thought he must be a poor wrecked soul,
Haunted to death by some wandering ghoul.

The stranger turned, and with fierce bright eye
Gleaming, half smiled at his stifled cry;
Looked till his soul quaked through and through,
Till his teeth were chattering, cheeks were blue.
"H'm! not worth having — a thing so small —
Far less to me than nothing at all!
But come along for a little space
It'll not be hard to find *you* a place!
A soul your size may be tucked away
In far less room than a seed of hay."

Solomon struggled with might and main
To speak — to call to Stephen — in vain!
He was swiftly raised, and borne away,
Far from the regions of light and day.
The blackness of darkness wrapped him round,
In freezing tortures his limbs were bound;
Then suddenly plunged in a world of flame,
Colder than ice he grew in the same.

"Welcome at last!" a voice at his ear
Sounded familiar — once had been dear.
"Brother, by you I might have been led
To choose a worthier life, instead
Of perishing, body and soul, at last,
When many a sorrow of life was past.
Slowly I fell — till I landed here!"

"Did ever I urge"—
    "You oft were near,
And, had you but shown some love for me,
I'd have followed you over land and sea."

"Did I ne'er ask you to give it up?"

"You laughed, at first, when I took the cup,"
Bitterly cried the sorrowful ghost,
"You whom I loved and honored the most.
And after — well, have you ever heard
Of one who's reformed by an angry word?"

"I never — no! I *never* have tried
To lead you, Brother, one inch aside —
(Oh, could I weep," he groaned to himself,
"But ghosts never weep — thou luckless elf.")
Solomon tried to touch his face,
But a thousand sparks flew off into space.

"Lead! nay you cared for yourself alone!
Soon, as a brother you would not own
A fellow who cherished a love for you
Like to a woman's, tender and true.
Alas! my brother, you threw aside
(Cherishing ever your worldly pride)
Opportunities, wooings of grace —
Past — impossible now to replace!

A life, though a hundred years it be,
Is but a speck in eternity.
Yet fadeless stands on the Book of Time
Each thought of the heart, each deed sublime,
Each tone of love, or murmur of woe,
Each tear of pity "—

"Oh, cease the flow
Of useless wisdom! — haunting me now
Are regrets for every broken vow.—
My hands are empty "—

"Nay! wait awhile!
Take of your darling gold, to beguile
The weary hours!" cried a mocking sprite.
"Here are guineas! fresh-coined guineas
 bright!
Cover him over! press down each palm!
What he loves best shall his soul embalm.
Coins all over him! — hammer them in! —
They can't be closer than sordid sin."

Whirling and laughing, each elf of flame
Turned rainbow colors, yet looked the same,

Then forward brought to his nearer view
A tiny creature of doubtful hue,
Shrunk, disfigured, and withered away,
A thing unfit for the light of day.

"What is it?" he groaned.
                        With gleeful shout
They turned the pitiful Thing about.
A terrible Voice was at his ear.
"Behold!—'tis thyself! henceforth with fear,
And dread remorse, shall it follow thee—
A weariless shadow! Now dost see
That spectre tall with the heavenward eyes—
As seeking the lights of Paradise?
See its airy robe, its kindly grace,
The noble thoughts that to many a race
Would be as the dew to mortal flowers,
Awaking to growth their heaven-born powers?
The hand outstretched to the poor, you see,
With words of love and of charity.
Peace on the brow, and joy in the heart,
For, strange as it seems, doth one impart.

Richer is he than if naught were given.
Wonderful! — still, 'tis the way of Heaven."

As the word was uttered there went a groan
Through the lurid caverns.
     "Great Unknown,"
Solomon murmured, "who was this man?"

"Thyself hadst thou but followed the plan
The mind of Wisdom had formed for thee."
"But now?"
     "Behold thy Eternity!
Hadst thou not fostered thy bosom sin
The other portrays what thou *mightst have been*.
Henceforth these phantoms thy steps shall haunt,
Nor leave at sound of thy stern 'avaunt'!
One pressing close to thy shrinking side,
And one, half seen, in the distance glide."

Solomon shuddered, and cried "O Fate!
Why torture a soul disconsolate?

Had I but dreamed of this depth of woe
Naught could have tempted my soul so low."

"Ignorance — was it? or love of pelf?
I say 'twas simply worship of self.
Who will not his brother's keeper be
Partakes of his sin and misery."

"And no repentance"—

      "The time is past!
The gates of Mercy are closed at last."—
Silent the voice.

     A garden appeared.
Solomon's heart at the sight was cheered.
He almost laughed as he plucked a peach
Temptingly hanging within his reach,
And quick to his fire-parched lips he pressed.
How hard! how heavy! Then sore distressed:
"Only painted gold!" he cried, "alas! —
And this bubbling stream is of molten glass!"

Before his eyes it melted away,
As a weeping soul approached to say,

"I'm a girl you turned out into the street
One night in a storm of wind and sleet.
I saw a palace of gilded sin —
It was warm and light, and I wandered in."

"You owed me the rent!" old Solomon said —
'Twas the force of habit, he felt, instead
Of the sordid heart which had shrunk away,
One throbbing anguish, and added, — "Nay!
The fault is mine! — I should suffer all —
I was the cause of your woful fall!
Sorrows of many lie at my door,
Weigh down my soul — I can bear no more —
God pity us both!"
                         A cry arose —
That sacred name 'mid his bitter foes!
But ent'ring in came a noted guest,
And the demons sped at their lord's behest.

Solomon fell with a ghastly grin —
He burned without, and he burned within;
The ice was melting, and flowed in tears
As he suffered on for a thousand years. —

Then suddenly came unlooked for peace,
A hopeful exit, a swift release!

On his way from the deep, submundane sphere
He saw an ethereal guide draw near,
Safely to lead him, through æons of space
To the distant planet his dwelling-place.

An hour or two they pleasantly spent
In viewing the glorious firmament,
But Solomon anxiously longed to see
The shores of Earth. "Though I need not," said he,
"Expect to greet a familiar face
Unless it be an exceptional case,—
They could not have lived such a number of years."

"Now look," said the guide, "where that mist appears."

"They're clouds on our Ocean! I see them plain —
I knew I should recognize home again!"

"Well — be not so eager! but wait and see
How things on the planet appear to me. —
Only a second or two, then we'll go
Wherever you please. — Now, then! look
 below."

Solomon's gaze on the Earth was bent.
"Why are the people so very intent?
Catching at bubbles which break in the hand —
Carrying loads of the heaviest sand —
Rags and tatters of gaudy hue —
Ancient books, worm-eaten through!"

Said his guide, "The heaviest load of pelf
That any man bears is his own dear self!"

"And why does each carry a looking-glass?
'Tis not alone the merry-eyed lass; —
Another odd thing! no glass reflects
Exactly the form one there expects."

Then the guide smiled — "No man is the
 same
In his own eyes — so worthy of blame —

As would be another were he untrue
To the light that shone within him. You
See in the glass what *they think* they are."

"Blissfully ignorant state — ha! ha!"
Solomon laughing turned to his guide,
Who shook his head, and sadly replied —
"Wilfully blind! they've a Counsellor
Would gladly aid them. They do not err
Helplessly hurried along by Fate."

"Some seem hastening — some of them wait,
Laughing and talking of nothing at all
But the veriest nonsense!—*minds so small*"—

"Wait!" said his guide, "let's see where *you* stand,
Or where you *stood* — with your golden sand."

Solomon cheerfully shook his head —
"I'm not so silly as *they* are," he said.

Patiently smiled the angel, his eye
Bright with the sunlight of charity.

"Let's see... you're a Christian? well look
  down
To the left. 'Professors' the half in town —
'Tis the one respectable thing to be,
So they all go in for the form you see.
There's many a good man fond of pelf,
And many a Christian good to himself —
Struggling for righteousness — and for ease,
And to enter the Kingdom as him may please.
Of course, in the truly-changed of heart,
Though the weeds may grow when they've
  got a start,
There's always a longing for better things —
Occasional draughts from God's fountain-
  springs —
And some so closely dwell in his grace
That their smiles seem reflections from God's
  own face.
There's no strict line, though many may
  search,
Dividing apart the World and the Church,
For some who outside lingering wait
Shall enter in at the Golden Gate;

While others, high up in Church's pale
Shall loudly knock, but an entrance fail!"

Says Solomon, "Oft to the church I went"—

"No doubt! and when for the prayer you
    bent
You thought of the rise in a favored stock;
Of rents coming in from a tenement block"—

"Not always!—you see for many a year
I'd my mother's prayers; and her parting tear
Was a pearl to me of a price untold —
Far richer than all the mines of gold!"

"And then?"—
           "A younger and fairer face
Won my devotion.— My lovely Grace!—
Her picture hangs in my dining-hall
Looking brightly down from the sombre wall.
But a few years passed — there came a morn
When I wept alone, for my love was gone!"
Silent he mused for a little space,
A look of sorrow altered his face —

Deeper the wrinkles that in by-gone years,
Had been the channels of bitter tears.

Gentle the light in his mentor's eyes
As he heard the old man's tender sighs.
"And you loved no more?" he softly said.

Solomon, shaking his bowed, gray head,
For a moment made to him no reply.
Then, looking up with remorseful eye,
"I've wronged myself, and I've wronged my
 child ;
My brain was turned, and my actions wild!
I didn't want her to marry at all,
But a fellow, handsome, and fair and tall,
Poor as poverty — that of course —
Won her by singing till he was hoarse
Of the 'beauties of love.' And so the two
Eloped! — Well, what could the creatures do?
Indeed, I had but myself to blame —
If 't been me I'd ha' done the same.
Well — from that time to me she's been dead.
There's not a day but my heart has bled,

Though I would not receive a single word,
And years have passed since her voice I've
    heard.
Though many a time to the house she came
The servants dared not mention her name;
Poor Stephen alone, has often plead
That I'd take back the cruel words I'd said.
I long to see her! — I scarce can wait —
But, oh! — no doubt I shall be too late!"

The guide, who had listened with patient grace,
Looked this way, and that. "Ah here's the
    place!
Come! this is the way for us to go
I've three choice sinners I want to show; —
Saintly sinners — two of the three —
"Of such shall the Kingdom of Heav'n *not*
    be."

" You're speaking now of those in the Church,
If you had asked me to join in the search
These would not compare to some I could
    find —
Criminals sunken in body and mind "—

"Those make no pretence, but God they face;
They sin and die, and go to their place.
This is a far more respectable kind,
Supposed to have conscience and cultured mind."

"These people seem to be much mixed up."

"That's Deacon Miles, with a silver cup,
And golden plate of the best of fare,
Complacently smiling.— The starving there,
With famished eyes on his pious face,
Hear, without heeding, his well-worn grace.
The Deacon swallows the lion's share,
Then scatters the crumbs with a lordly air,
And the crowd applaud — at his 'charity!'"

"Good sakes!" cried Solomon, "just to see—"

"Look here," said his guide, "here's another saint,
They can only see the enamel and paint,
The reddened lips, and the darkened eyes —
Here's a candidate for Paradise!

Delicate cambric and costly lace,
Silks and satins and jewels, grace
A form that to men seems fair to see,
But a spirit warped for Eternity!
See her winning smile, her gracious air —
All put on for the company there.
See her again as she stands alone.
A poor girl comes with piteous moan, —
'Tis the seamstress pale whom a bill she owes
For weeks of work on her elegant clothes.
She answers, "Why, *really!* — you've come too late!
I'm going to church — so you'll have to wait.
I've only a single piece of gold —
That the contribution plate must hold!"
Solomon turning his head away
Put his hand in his pocket the girl to pay. —
Nothing was there, so he turned again
And fixed his eyes on a group of men
Surrounding a coffin, narrow and small.
He shuddered! — for under the velvet pall
His own form filled the allotted space,
And he sadly gazed on his own dead face.

The group around were not very sad —
In fact they seemed to be soberly glad,
But every spot they could possibly drape
Was hung with the richest, deepest of crape.
Solomon saw in the heart of each
Some thoughts quite opposed to the measured speech.

"What sinful waste!" thought Tabitha Shrew.
"I should say those men had little to do
To spend so much in making a spread —
Should all have been for the heirs instead."
Silent and sad, with occasional sighs,
She pressed a handkerchief to her eyes.

"I wonder how much we'll all get 'round,"
Mused spendthrift Dick with eyes on the ground;
While cousin Anne, the richest of all,
Smoothing a crease in the heavy pall,
Placing the flowers with exquisite taste,
Wished that the bearers would make more haste!

SOLOMON GRINDER'S CHRISTMAS EVE.   35

Thought no more of the one who lay dead,
But greatly longed the Will should be read.

Solomon noted each jealous eye.—
There was not a tear, nor a heart-felt sigh,
In all this pomp of funereal gloom.

But hark!—a sound from another room,—
There wept old Stephen! Nor was he alone,
For through the sobs came a tender tone.

"O, Nellie, he never knew Jesus, dear,
Or he'd have loved us when he was here—
Jesus loved children *so well*, you know."

"But tell me, sister, where did he go?
Mama keeps crying the livelong day—
I 'spect she's sorry he's gone away."

Solomon nodded his head to the guide,
Who, kindly smiling, came to his side.
"Stephen's grandchildren?"
                "Nay! but your own!"
"But Stephen said"—
                "Let Stephen alone

For finding a way to blind your eyes! —
Noble of heart — though not very wise."

Solomon wept. He remembered well
The same sweet tones of his darling Nell.

" Look once again."

"Why! — there's the poor girl! —
And there's Cousin Anne. Ha! many a curl
And fuss and furbelow she's got on!
What's that? — she calls to her coachman,
 "John!"
Ah! the seamstress pale has fall'n in the street,
And lies quite still near the horses' feet!
Drive on! proud lady — why — no! she's
 out!
The sleeves of lace are folded about
The clean, patched clothes, while the faded
 hat
On her shoulder rests! Now what's she at?
That's not her daughter?"

"Oh, no! — you see
Her heart is melted in charity.

And then — she thinks with a throe of fear

'So might it be with my children dear!'"

"I thought that her heart was puffed with
    pride."

"Ah, yes! *you* looked on only *one side!*
There's no one perfect — never will be,
But *no* one is wholly bad you see;
The lightest head in Vanity Fair
Has other thoughts than of what to wear.
That girl's misfortune has won a friend
Who will spare no pain to the goodly end
Of making her happy,— the truth to prove,
Who giveth truly giveth in love."

"There is that spendthrift Dick, I declare!
With sorry hat, and disordered hair.
He stops to enter a restaurant —
Why, what a poor little figure, gaunt,
Creeps up and puts in a famine plea!
Says Dick, 'I guess you're worse off than me,
So take this quarter, poor little scamp —
The last I've got!' he mutters, 'a tramp,

And luckless sinner, sure I was born!'
Poor boy!" said Solomon, "how forlorn
And reckless he looks!— yet there's some good
In spite of his foolish hardihood.—
I'll rub my specs!— must be going wild!
Tabitha nursing a poor sick child?
— And old Deacon Miles — why *bless* my life!
Kind as can be to a bed-rid wife!"

On the angel's face was a smile, and a tear,
As the woman prayed for her "husband dear;"
Fearing and trembling lest, being "so good,"
He'd die and leave her in solitude!

— "The thief that stole my watch t'other day
Pawns it his mother's bread bill to pay,
And every article he can spare
Gives to a friend who has less to wear!
— That hungry child — gives the crust in her hand
To the little one! — I understand —

Why! — am I alone? — yes — so it seems" —

Solomon came from the land of dreams
With a quivering cry, of "Oh! Oh dear!"
And his neck was stiff, and his sight was blear;
But he struggled to rise, and gazed around,
Then heaved a sigh of relief profound.

"Why, master dear," came the piping tone
Of the faithful Stephen, "here all alone,
You'd like to have set yourself on fire —
Why you're hot as a blacksmith's wagon tire."

"H'm! h'm," said Solomon, scratching his head,
"Not half so hot as if I'd been dead!"

"Been — *what?*" cried Stephen, taken aback,
"He's out of his head, — alack! — alack!"
And raised a pitcher of water straight
To cool off the fever.
                    "Hold, Stephen — wait!
I'm no more crazy than you. — Sit down,
It's only a *dream.*"

"How very brown
Your knees is," said Stephen, "little more
'D ha' burnt you up like an ole pine door.
Well — Smith's out here — will you let him
    come?
He says he ' 'lowed he'd find you to hum,'
Some how he don't seem willin' to leave,
And says to mind you it's Christmas Eve."

Solomon looked at the kind old man
As if bewildered. Then he began
To ask some questions, and smiling in space
Cracked every wrinkle over his face,
As hope and joy in his heart awoke.

The clock ticked loudly. 'Twas on the stroke
Of nine, as Solomon quickly 'rose,
And put on his coat.
              — "Master! — it snows!
Besides, it's gettin' pow'fully late —
Well! well! I never! — he wouldn't wait;
He'll come back chilled, I'll venture to say,
And then there'll be — well — *something* to
    pay."

Busily Stephen swept up the room
With the small remains of an ancient broom,
Arranged the fire with the nicest care,
And soon had the tea-kettle boiling there.

"Of course he'll scold," the little man said,
"But then he mustn't go cold to bed.—
He shall have some toast and hot spiced
 wine.
Ha! now these fire-irons brightly shine.
Oh, yes!' to the picture, "you may smile,
But you'll have to *wait* for a little while.
It'll all come right in time, I doubt —
How those eyes do follow one all about!
It's warm an' comfortin', I'll sit down;
I reckon he'll soon be back from town."

The wild wind whistling, noisy and shrill,
Rattled the windows and doors with a will;
Feathery snow down the chimney came,
But hissing flew from the angry flame.
"A Christmas hard for the sick and poor,"
Groaned Stephen, peeping out from the door,

"An' I jist say it's reely a sin
For folks to be out that orter be in!
There's no use talkin'! — I'm that distressed
About old Master, I jist *can't* rest."
And so, with many a mutt'ring sound,
Stephen kept wandering round and round.

And where was Solomon? At the door
He met the Smith he had snubbed before,
And merely saying, "Come 'long with me,"
Walked off like a stripling of twenty-three,
Giving poor Smith such a shock of surprise
That he just stood still with staring eyes,—
Then followed on in a swinging trot,
Wondering painfully whether or not
The "ole man rightly was in his head?"
At any rate not a word was said
Till Solomon Grinder turned about,
Putting his other thoughts to rout
By saying, "Look here, my worthy friend —
Why — what's the matter? — I wish you'd
    attend."

For the man stood off for a goodly space,
Astonishment painted on his face,
And wondered if he were really there,
Or taking a ride on a wild night-mare.
Solomon laughed. It was odd to hear!
The first of the kind for many a year.
Then he approached him — but Smith retired
As quick as if a gun had been fired!
Look here!" growled Solomon, "where's the rent?
I'll wager my hat it's all been spent!"
Quite re-assured, Smith came to his side,
To plead excuses eagerly tried.
"You see, your Honor, my wife's been sick,
An' ther' ain't a right well child nor chick.—
Mebbe it's wantin' enough to eat,
Or mebbe the lack o' coal fer heat,
I d'clare I dunno! — but — here's every cent
We'd scratched fer Christmas, towards the rent."
The large thin hand, stretched out in the cold,
Could hardly the much-prized savings hold.

Solomon, taking it, also took note
Of the worn-out shoes and ragged coat.

"I'm sure I wouldn't my duty shirk,
But I don't seem pow'ful strong to work.—
The times is hard," with a weary sigh.

Solomon, doubtful what reply
Might best suit the case, made answer then,
"Much depends on the kind of men —
Or people — and their strength to endure.
'The times' seem always hard to the poor."
His voice was gentle,— yes, even sad,
And, as they walked, the other was glad
To speak of his sad mistakes in life,
Of his little children, and patient wife;
Of the baby lost, and their anxious search,
And the crippled boy who sang in the church;
Of little Jane who, but four years old,
Was the mother's nurse, and with care untold
Tenderly watched her early and late,
Yet looked for 'Pa' at the garden gate.
"It hardly would seem like home to me
If she wasn't waiting there, you see."

So, being drawn on, his drift of speech
Pictured the thoughts and wishes of each.
"Look here," said Solomon, "here's a store —
You've nothing to do for an hour or more?"

"Why — no, sir! — if there's aught I can do
I'll be mightily glad to work fer you,
If you'll tell me what you please to want."

"I'm going into this restaurant —
Just come along!" for the poor man stood
Shaking and chattering do what he would.
"Well — if *you* won't go there — *I* shall not!
I'm almost *perished* for something hot."

Without a word Smith followed him in,
Though with glistening eye, and quivering
    chin,
"Oh dear!" said he, "but *don't* it smell *good*?
It's most as nice as eatin' the food!"
He laughed.
        Something ailed Solomon's throat.
He turned away — unbutt'ning his coat.

"Now waiter," said he, "if you are through,
Bring your hottest coffee and steak for two.
And be in a hurry! it's getting late,
And hungry people don't like to wait."

"All right, sah! — your table — latest news —
Read while you're waitin', sah, — if you
 choose."

Five minutes, an age to Smith, went by.
Now smoking viands before him lie —
But not for long, for his head is bent
To give his craving hunger content.
But, slyly, he over half of it hid
Within his pocket. Solomon bid
The waiter fill up another plate,
And Smith thought kindlier of his fate —
Felt better able to cope with men,
And struggle on with his life again.

"Well, now," says Solomon, in the street,
"We'll have to hasten, for time is fleet,

And I have several things to do,—
And several errands, too, for you.
I'm glad that I wrote these notes to-night.—
My Brother and Dick, and my old clerk, White,
Who crippled himself at the store; and Nan,
My mother's old servant,— a right good plan —
Just a line or two of greeting to each,—
Perhaps the checks will be better than speech.
Where are we now?— oh, here is the store.—
Could you work for me for a month or more?
— Here is a box. So! the letters are in.
Ha! ha!— they'll wonder — dear! dear! what a din
That band keeps up! Well, what do you say?
We'll talk to-morrow about the pay."

Smith, glancing down at his dingy clothes
Said, " I ain't much proud as Poverty knows."

" Oh, if that's all! — we'll look out for that.—
Mr. Clothier, fit this man with a hat.

You've ready-made clothes? So! that's all
    right,
Fix him warmly — fit for to-night.
Shoes? yes,— and mittens! — Why, never
    mind!
A way of repaying you're sure to find."

For the man was struggling hard for speech,
But suitable words seemed out of reach.

"There's always a way for the man who *wills*,
If he goes it strong in spite of ills. —
Go put on your clothes — my soul is vexed
To see you suffering! —

                    Well, what next,"
He mused as he waited down by the door.
"Let's see! — ha! Stephen's clothes are so
    poor —
And mine! ha! ha! Well this will not do.
I'll order a suit — no! I'll call for two —
This is no weather for clothes so light. —
Oh — could I but see my Nell to-night!
Ten years! — God pity my flinty heart,
And forgive the grudge which kept us apart.

Little by little I sunk so low
As the miserly spirit began to grow. —
Where is she now? — oh! Stephen can tell,
I'll ask him to-night — my darling Nell!
Ready? all right. — This order please fill,
And send the things as soon as you will.
What kind of a fit? — oh, never fear —
You've had my measure this many a year —
Though you've forgotten me. There's the
    name."

"If they're not just right" —
              "You'll not be to blame.
I haven't an atom of time to spare —
Send of the best that you have for wear."

"All right, sir."
      "Good-night."
          "Good-night."
                  "— Dear me!
What a loss of time! — now Smith, you'll see
These orders for coal and loaves of bread
Given out to these people — as I have
    said?"

"Surely!" said Smith, as he touched his hat,
"You may trust me the same as yourself for that."
His deep voice trembled — perhaps with cold;
"May you be — repaid — a thousand-fold."

"Too much set down on the other page."
Solomon shook his head like a sage.
"Now, as you'll have money to work for me
Here's some in advance. Good-night!" and he
Hastened off down the street all thanks to shun.

"Queer old duffer!" cried clerk number one
In the store they had left, "no end of larks
To polish him off."

"Ah — Mr. Marks!
If I'd his power with a scratch of a pen
I'd soon be on top of the pile again! —
Tell you, sir, money's the one great thing,
It's the lever that weights the puppet string.

Think of the power that he's packed away!—
That's Grinder, the miser!"
                              "You don't say!
I'll be more respectful to his gray hairs.
I wonder if he has any heirs!"

The storm had ceased. The pale moonlight
Shone soft on the snow, all pure and white,
Soon to be trodden, or swept aside,
To melt away in the swollen tide;—
As many a soul from the country home
Into the city will careless roam,
And lose its beauty and freshness there,
Far from the joy of its native air.
Solomon thinks not of this, his eye
Roams here and there, he could scarce tell
    why.
"Such a lot of snow for so late begun!"

"Now, Nellie, this is the prettiest one!"
Cried a childish voice that made him start,—
Pressing a hand to his throbbing heart.

"Stephen's grand-children? — no! — my own!
My darling's face, and her very tone
In childish joy. Why have I not guessed
When Stephen showed them — at his behest!
Those lovely eyes! — that beautiful hair
So brown, yet with sunlight imprisoned there.
That look familiar — I know not what —
Nobody else in the world has got."

They stood at a window filled with toys —
Wonderful things for girls and boys,
Dollies were there who could dance and sing;
Beautiful china — and everything
Brilliant, and lovely, to please the eye. —
Much of it only the rich could buy.
But there, pressed closely against the glass,
Were a dozen faces. One little lass,
Habited poorly — as all the rest —
Laughed and chattered with joyous zest.

"Lillie! but see that boy with a drum!
And those china dolls! will Santa Claus come
And fill our stockings with bu'f'lest things —
Lovely angels with little gold wings?

Lots of candies and nuts and cake "—

" And what for Mama?"

"Oh, she shall take
The big-est and best-est of all that's there —
You know we *always* save Mama *her* share!
Will he come?"

The other made reply
Sweet and tender, a tear in her eye,
"If mother *could*, we should have them all
To make us happy!— O — see! that small
Old gentleman hears us!— Come let's run!
It's getting *so* late,— we've had lots of fun!"
So clasping hands they had turned away
When Solomon called to them.

"Stay! dears, stay!
All of you little ones come with me
We'll go inside and see — what we'll see."

Delighted they all accept the plan
And follow the "funny old gentleman,"
Up to the counter, quiet as mice.
Solomon heading them, asked the price
Of various articles,

"Seems to *me*
The very best plan would likely be,"
Said the sage, red-headed, kind young clerk,
Nodding his head with a funny jerk,
"To give so much to each little elf,
And set it off to choose for itself!"

So Solomon thought, but kept the girls,
Lillie and Nell, with hands on their curls,
Questioned them softly about their home.—
Had they no father that they should roam
Abroad so late?
Then they sadly told
He'd died when Nellie was five years old,
And the mother had sewed till the day before,
But had told them now she could do no more.

Solomon Grinder turned quite pale,
And had to hold to the counter rail.

"We hated the dear Mama to leave,
But *she* said to come — it was Christmas Eve!
So — though it *was* stormy — out we came.—
Do you think we're very much to blame?"

SOLOMON GRINDER'S CHRISTMAS EVE. 55

"No! No!— have you plenty at home to eat?"

Lillie answered him, brave and sweet,
"We've nothing at all, but Mama said
We've the same God that the birdies fed."

Then Solomon spoke with a thankful heart,
As the little ones made as if to start,
"No longer my darlings shall hungry be!—
Now all you little folks — follow me!—
But first, Mr. Clerk— choose quick my dears,
Well! Well! they cannot tell *what*, it appears,
Would please them best!—here's a dollar— no *two*,
And, one for yourself — just wrap up a few
Of the things they fancy. Good-night."
                                      "Good-night,
And thank you heartily!"
                                      "That's all right!"
Solomon laughed, but with tender heart.
"Come all you babies — now for a start!"

Full many a backward glance they threw,
But followed on into "pastures new."

Then into the baker's shop, next door,
With fully a hungry dozen more,
Solomon hastened, with child-like joy.
"Two buns apiece for each girl and boy.

Each left clasping a loaf of bread,
And a sack of riches the size of his head —
Candy and nuts — and the precious toys —
Who could describe their Christmas joys!

Solomon home with his darlings went,
His mind quite filled with its glad intent,
He found a welcome so true, and deep,
That, what did he do, but sit and weep!

The children, climbing upon his knee,
Gave kisses of love and sympathy;
While his daughter pressed his hand in her
    own,
And gladdened his heart with her tender tone.

SOLOMON GRINDER'S CHRISTMAS EVE. 57

The bells are ringing! 'tis Christmas morn!
So many years since the Christ was born!
Well may our hearts, and our tongues, rejoice,
The Lord in Heaven can hear each voice,
And read the love of our souls, and bless
Our loved and ourselves with happiness.

Solomon Grinder, in lonely state,
Sat, and looked at the very same plate
He honored so when our tale began,—
The plate was the same, but not the man.

Stephen had worn a bewildered look
For the last two hours. His master took
Delight in saying the oddest things
About "seeing angels, minus the wings."
And then the provisions! what a store
Of things had arrived the night before!
And why should the table, this morn, be set
For four! — and the best that they could get!

Rap! rap! rap!
        "Stephen, some one is there,"—
Solomon laughing rose from his chair.

"Pray open the door!"—

It backward flew!—
Two lovely children came into view—
Running to Solomon, clasped him tight,
Laughing in ecstacy of delight!

"O Master, dear, *don't* be angry — *please*,"
Cried Stephen, falling upon his knees,
"Here's your dear daughter — Mistress Nell."

Solomon smiled as it pleased him well.
"Get up! old friend.— the greatest surprise
Is that which looks from your dull old eyes."
And his own were moist,—"I've done a wrong,
I own to it now. Ah, the days were long"—
"Nay, father, dear, what is sad, forget!
Many the days of happiness yet
Together, I trust. Though the sun *be* low
We'll rejoice in the light *of the after glow!*"

Solomon Grinder is not a saint,
(Touching his portrait with outline faint),
Though in Charity's rank a strong recruit,
Sweetened and mellowed like ripened fruit,

And strictly honest as man can be,
He's fond of money, as one may see.
Still, you may read, in his changing face,
The outward marks of a growth in grace.

His daughter ministers peace and love,
And speaks of the joys of the home above.
Her children are growing lovely and tall,
Like the roses climbing the garden wall.

Old Stephen sits in his easy chair,
Rheumatic and patient, without a care;
Taking life's sunshine along with the rain,
Accepting its bounties, its beauties, its pain,
As gifts direct from a Father, kind,
And tender, and gracious! Not resigned
Like some — with lifted brows and a sigh,
But with thankful heart, right cheerfully.

We may not judge of the charity,
Or miserly heart, of others, but we
May taste of the purest joy that's given,
By entering into the labors of Heaven, —

Labors of love, and ministry,
Words of the tenderest sympathy.
Not every one has the power of gold,
But better than that, *a thousand-fold*,
The strength of heart, and clearness of eye,
To see and hail Opportunity;
Nor backward glance with regretful sigh,
When, with sails unfurled, she has passed
  them by.
Where a marriage is, how many rejoice!
There are fewer weep at the mourner's voice.
Remember — and give of the light, thine
  own,
To her who sitteth in darkness alone.
The *way* of giving, more than the *gift*,
May a needy, sorrowful heart uplift;
While a bird of joy is warbling there
Whose notes sound not on the summer
  air.
We will let the frailties of others be
Hid by a mantle of Charity,
And kindly speak, for, happen what will,
Our erring brother 's our brother still!

O willing hand, and O tender heart,
Who gladly doth to thy friend impart —
Thy friend, whoever hath greater need, —
At this blessed season we say "God speed,
And shine on thy life, as the Star on them,
Who sought for the Babe in Bethlehem."

My Conscience and I.

I stood at the gate of my Conscience,
    She gazed at me from the door,
Then hastened along the pathway —
    As oft she had done before.

It was early in life's fair spring-time,
    The flowers were lovely to see,
And the birds of hope and promise
    Sang gaily from every tree;

But my heart was heavy within me,
    For my Mentor's brow was sad,
And I missed the smile of welcome
    That often had made me glad.

Then I saw in her eyes reflected
    My wayward and foolish life,
And resolved, in my youthful fervor,
    To engage in a nobler strife.

MY CONSCIENCE AND I.

The years passed on. I was prospered,
   And rose to some wordly fame,
And many a great transaction
   Had sanction of my good name.

My Conscience, all uninvited,
   Would whisper soft in my ear,
'Till, angry, I turned and left her
   Determined I would not hear;

I would win in every battle,
   Whether weal or woe betide.
But, at last, in the midst of sorrow,
   Was lowered my haughty pride!

I knocked at the door of my Conscience.
   Unanswered, I glanced within;
There lay she, starving and dying —
   Alas! my neglect and sin!

Oh, I will — but no! my *actions*
   Shall tell, — not an empty word.
And I went among my people
   As one whose heart had been stirred.

And the widows and orphans blessed me,
  But my millions grew no less,
So I sought the country over
  For those who were in distress.

I gave not my voice for the strongest
  But the one I thought was right;
And to those who groped in darkness
  I gladly offered a light.

Now, at many an humble fireside,
  Which Heaven by my hand has blessed,
Dwell smiling Peace and Contentment
  Instead of a sad unrest.

And my Conscience, sitting beside me,
  For that is her place alway,
Is smiling, and I am happy, —
  Nearing heaven from day to day.

Song of the Zephyr.

Where the dew glistens
　On mountain high,
Bathed in its brightness
　There, there am I!

Waking the echoes
　In woodland glade,
Laughing in chorus
　With mountain maid.

Roses and lilies
　Bend to my sigh,
Rapt in their sweetness
　There, there am I!

Hovering over
　The couch of distress,
Kissing the mourner
　In tenderness.

Breathing in music,
  Each early morn,
" Praise to Creator,"
  Through Alpine horn.

Catch of my fragrance,
  Upward I fly,
Wrapped in a sunbeam
Sweetly to die!

PURIFIED.

By anguish, that from out the weak heart crushes
   The little life that bore it on its way,
The strong heart stronger grows, while onward rushes
   The force resistless, without stop or stay!
   As when a raging tempest hath its sway,
The slender weaklings scatter o'er the land,
While century oaks in conscious grandeur stand.

What are these moments to eternal spaces!
   Be strong, tho' suffering, for the surgeon's steel
By pain is guided to the ulcerous places —
   The strong hand, tender, wounds thee but to heal.
   Tho' in thine inmost, hidden life, thou feel

The cautery applied, yet surely know
The tissues of thy heart shall purer grow.

Patience, dear soul, tho' the fierce fire be burning,
  Melting like wax the ore within thine heart,
Thoughts and desires, and hopes and fears, o'erturning,
  Sending in fumes away the baser part;
  Shrink not! but bear the purifying smart.
Know, that the Lord who loves thee well, would see
The image of Himself, reflect in thee.

From out the ashes of thy dead self, glowing,
  A better life shall Phœnix-like appear;
And fairer, and more God-like ever growing,
  Shall on fleet pinions to the Light draw near;
  Shall walk with God, and feel nor pain, nor fear,
(As in the happy days of Eden story),
And, like the moon, shine with reflected glory.

LEAVING THE FARM.

YES, neighbor, I reckon I'll leave ye,—
    Tomorrer the tenant comes in!
So stay, and set down awhile with me,
    Fer p'raps I'll not see ye ag'in.
What? ye won't sit? then come in the orchard
    Ther's some cheers by the old apple tree.—
Here 'tis.—Yes!—A mighty sight bigger
    Than when planted by Polly and me!

Ye mind when we moved in this homestid,
    How the woods come most up to the door?
It took us a day to go millin',
    And 'twas miles upon miles to a store.
My Polly she sung in the spring-house,
    And sung as she spun at her yarn,
While I was away at my ploughin'
    Or threshin' the wheat in the barn!

What a sweet gentle mother was Polly!
  Yet she raised up her childern by rule,
And took 'em all with her to meetin',
  And sent them as reg'lar to school.
And the childern they took so to learnin'
  They must go away from the farm —
You know, neighbor Jones, how they left us,
  But, thank God! they come to no harm!

'*Twas* hard when we give up the youngest, —
  For the next one hed died when a man,
You remember, — but he was so earnest
  We give up our own happy plan.
For, somehow, I fully hed reckoned
  I'd give up the homestid to him —
He was al'ays so good to his Mother. —
  Neighbor, my eyes's kinder dim —

These spectacles must need a rubbin'. —
  There — now they'll do better I know.
The boys was so set on my leavin'
  I couldn't do nothin' but go.

But here were our joys, and our sorrers,
    And you know that we worked with a will,
But my Polly,— she sings with the angels,
    And her busy hands— now they are still.

The hardest of all is to leave her,
    And the childern that sleeps at her side. —
Oh, yes! neighbor, — I know they be risen,
    But this is the place where they died.
And sometimes when I set in the fire-light,
    A-thinking of those still so dear,
They seem to be coming around me,
    And puttin' the'r hands on my cheer.

And sometimes I go over yonder,
    And work with the flowers, or the sod
That covers the graves of my Polly,
    And the childern that's livin' with God.

And soon by their side I'll be restin' —
    For the boys has agreed I shall come —
So livin', or dyin', you'll see me
    Return to the blessed old home.

Do they say the wagon's a-waitin'?
  Oh, well then, I s'pose I must go,
For the boys'll be lookin' for "Father,"
  And I must look happy you know!
Oh, yes, I *am* blessed in my childern,
  They're lovin' and kind as kin be,
Good bye! and you'll — sometimes look yonder,
  And think of my Polly and me?

LEAD ME.

"Stay! let me lead you, darling,
    The way is rough and wild."
'Twas thus a tender father
    Addressed his wayward child.

"Oh, no! I'll pluck the roses
    So sweet, and lilies fair,—
All, all around is beauty,
    No harm can touch me there!"

But sharp thorns pierced her fingers,
    The rough stones bruised her feet,
Falling amid the briers,
    Her heart with woe replete,

Weeping, and sorely wounded,
    She took the offered hand;—
"Father, forgive, and help me!
    Alone I *cannot* stand."

'Tis thus, methought, in treading
　　The untried ways of Life.
The tempting flowers of pleasure,
　　With hidden poison rife,

Allure toward death and darkness
　　The children of the King.
Yet when they turn to seek Him,
　　With sad heart, sorrowing,

His hand is ever ready
　　To aid, to soothe, to bless;
To lead them on in gladness,
　　In peace and righteousness.

Dear Father, kind and watchful,
　　Keep thou my hand in thine.
Oh, that my life may praise Thee!
　　Thy love be ever mine.

A Garden.

Our souls are flowers
　Watered by heavenly dew,
In sunlit hours
　Growing,—'mid darkness too.

Many a rose,
　Radiant and beautiful,
Heavenward grows
　Thornless and dutiful.

Tiny stars, blue,
　Smile by the humble cot;
Loving and true
　Is the forget-me-not.

Happy and gay
　Tulips and poppies bright;
Cheerful alway,
　Heart's-ease, the heart's delight.

Lilies most fair
   Peace and security
Breathe in Heaven's air —
   Emblems of purity.

O for a life
   Like the sweet violet,
With fragrance rife,—
   Even in dying,— yet,

All through the days,
   Hidden in modesty,
Brightening Earth's ways,
   Making them fair to see.

O may one spot
   Brighter and better be,
Than had I not
   Bloomed in Eternity.

TRANSITION.

As the sweet day descending
  Calls to the night from far;
Heaven with the earth seems blending,
  Brightens life's evening star.
Through the shadowy valley
  Flowers of hope most sweet,
Mingling their perfume and beauty,
  Blossom around our feet.

So with the words Thy children
  Utter, on bended knee,
And in their songs of devotion
  Breathing their love to Thee; —
Like a sweet incense rising,
  Borne on the wings of prayer, —
So, for the soul, bound heavenward,
  Forming a golden stair.

Softly the shadows are gath'ring
  Over our joy, or woe,

Tender fingers of angels
  Guide our steps as we go.
Falt'ring we follow life's pathway,
  Oft-times our footsteps roam —
Dim eyes closed to the radiance
  Drawing us gently home.

Now the shadows are deep'ning!
  Day must be near at hand.
Cool is the tide, and fitful,
  Laving life's ebbing sand.
Far away are the murmurs
  Of the world's tempestuous sea, —
Its joys, its temptations, its sorrows;
  Its discords, its harmony.

Is there a mist on the river?
  What's on the other side?
Am I alone in the darkness?
  One step — into — the tide. —
Oh! what a glorious vision
  Opens before mine eyes!
This is the "Land Elysian." —
  I am in Paradise!

DRIFTING.

WE are drifting, ever drifting
   Down the swollen stream of time,
And the scenes of life are shifting —
   Like a wondrous pantomime.
We are passing down the river,
Soon to reach the great forever,
Where all bonds of earth will sever
        To the free.
See! the veil is gently lifting,
As we all are onward drifting
        To the sea.

Many little barks are gliding
   Side by side toward destined goal —
Some whose inmates are deriding
   Every interest of the soul,—

Seek in joy each passing pleasure,
Waste their love on earthly treasure,
Idle mirth's voluptuous measure —
   Do not see
Rocks beneath the waves are hiding,
Scarce a moment them dividing
   From the sea.

Genius, with the eyes of beauty,
 Waits not on the tardy stream,
Thinks not on the way of duty,
 Lives but in a glorious dream;
Oars of pleasure quickly seizes,
Courts the wild poetic breezes,
Music weird his fancy pleases,
   And to be
Where the rapids strong are dashing,
O'er the rocks of vengeance splashing,
And the waves their heads are lifting
As he madly on is drifting
   To the sea.

Some, with bright eyes raised are gliding,
  Watching oft a beauteous star,
Them unto the haven guiding
  By its influence from afar;
And with love their eyes are shining,
Glorious things they seem divining,
Every sense and thought refining.
            Melody
Sweet as sung by angels, ever,
Greets them, as they leave the river
            For the sea.

Onward drifting! may the pilot
  Who can steer our barks aright,
Guide us kindly to the islet
  Ere the coming of the night!
For the streams together blending,
Murmur, "Life to you is ending —
For you quickly are descending,
            And shall be
Where the cloud is surely lifting,
And your little barks be drifting,
            On the sea!"

REST.

Overcome with wearisome care,
And burdens too heavy to bear,
While the fingers, and heart, and brain
All re-echo the sad refrain,—
 "Rest! rest!—no rest
 For heart or brain oppressed!"

Laid aside from the toils of life,
Aside from its pleasures and strife,
There is heard the ebb and the flow
Of the human tide far below,—
 "Rest! rest!—oh, where
 Is rest from pain and care?"

Though the heart, and the pulses fail,
Though the face grow wan and pale;
In the eyes comes the Heavenly light
Of a Faith which grows more bright—

"Rest! rest! how sweet!"
Learning at Jesus' feet!

Only waiting the Master's will,
Sweetly bearing each passing ill;
As the breath, and the heart-beat, cease,
On the brow is the seal of Peace.
Rest! rest! — sweet rest!
Sleeping on Jesus' breast.

CHANGE.

A CHAUTAUQUA VALEDICTORY.

As a cloud-picture from the summer heaven
  Evanisheth our life from Earth away!
Our deeds sand-castles seem, all quickly riven—
  Obliterated by the tide-waves play.
The ceaseless tide of Time from day to day
  Rolls murmuring o'er all the spoils of men;
And wealth and honors, fame and grand display,
  Forgotten, sink to nothing back again.
O Force resistless, without stop or stay,
We quivering bow, and yield us as we may!

Thou glorious Solomon, to whom 'twas given
  To know great wisdom, and to feel great woe;—
To wander peaceful by the brook at even,
  Again, to doubt of all above, below,—

What now remains of all thy wondrous show?
  We know not if thine erring soul was shriven!
Nor where the hand which great gifts could bestow,
  Or, at a wave, condemn, or sign forgiven!
Thy once proud cities, silent in the glow
Of orient sunrise, lie, abased and low.

Ye great Assyrians of boundless power!
  Where are the riches that ye had in trust?
As lowland mists ye lived your little hour,—
  Then back resolved into untitled dust!
Your splendid palaces, the moth and rust,
  Red-handed war, the court, and ladies' bower,
All waste have laid; while mighty engine thrust
  Hath dashed to wreck each Babylonian tower.
Gone, as they ne'er had been, your pride and lust,
Your gorgeous pageants, and your souls distrust.

The silent centuries around your grave
  Circling, look down with wondrous starry
    eyes!
No power have they the mold'ring Past to
    save,
  But, sighing o'er the "has been," as it lies,
Each rosy palm, or withered, softly vies
  To bury deep the ashes of the brave,
The gay, the beautiful, the old and wise, —
  The palace and the hovel,— 'neath a wave
Of shimmering sand. All after destinies
Are sealed within God's Book of Mysteries.

Stupendous buildings all along the Nile
  Rear broken fronts, and many a temple
    vast,
In dread magnificence, a lordly pile,
  Speaks eloquently of the varied past.
Yet, tenantless and lone, they stand at last,
  Memorials of the doom, that shall, ere while,
Its poison blight o'er this fair Present cast,
  And walk resistless up each storied aisle!

Yet faith must like the Pyramids stand fast,
Calm as the Sphinx, nor backward shrink aghast!

Old Troy and Carthage fell, as ancient Greece;
  And Roman Consuls, longing for a name,
Woke many a land from out its dreams of peace,
  A million lives were nought so won they fame!
And Emp'rors rose, and it was still the same,
  The whole world sighed, but carnage might not cease;
Rome fell! and, after fearful sack and flame,
  Sat humbly waiting on through centuries.
Then other Emp'rors lived, and conquerors came,
  And solemn played their part in Life's short game.

How, worn and fretted by the tossing sea,
  The shores of Empires fall beneath its hand,

While, from its bosom, countries, soon to be,
  Volcanoes form from what was buried land.
A little world may be each grain of sand!
  Millions of lives form every coral key.—
And still the stars move on in orbits grand,
  The angels singing to their harmony!
While the sea moans upon the silvery strand,
And strains to break from out its mystic band.

Has life no recompense? Must dark-winged night,
  Enfolding silently each dwelling place,
Shut us forever out from hope and light,—
  Ruthlessly crushing out the human race?
Poor soul, come forth with me a little space
  Out of thy darkness! There are regions bright
Within the realms of Hope; and love and grace,
  Enough to fill each soul with keen delight.

Time's fading pictures God's hand shall retrace;
Eternity her treasures shall replace.

The jeweled fane of heathen devotee;
    The oak which bears the ivy on its breast;
The peasant wife with babe upon her knee,
    The lordly worldling with his arms and crest,—
All, all shall 'mid the dust be laid to rest.
    Those patriot hearts who strove their land to free;
No more in deadly strife their wrongs contest,
    But by the tyrant's side, all tranquilly,
Sleep well! no more with woes or sins depressed;
'Tis mystery! but God knows what is best.

And what, O friends! shall be our destiny?
    Each star that forms our Circle,— shall it shine,
Sparkle, and scintillate, 'till others be
    Self-lucent as the diamonds in the mine?

Or, if translucent, may a light divine
   Make fair, and pure, and full of charity,
The way we show to others! As a line
   True to our purpose; from earth tarnish free.
"Excelsior!" be our motto. Joys combine
To bless the worshipers at wisdom's shrine.

The treasures of the years are gathered in!
   Past is the harvest. — Is it great, or small?
Each be the judge! Ennobling 'tis to win
The sacred crumbs of learning as they fall
From tables of the wise. — Dear friends I call
   To say "good bye!" no more as they have been,
Shall loved ones gather in this pleasant hall.
   Ah! words would fail me should I but begin
To ope my heart to you. — But this recall,
"Farewell! a kind farewell!" I bid you all.

THE BEAUTIFUL SOUL.

"An angel to open the pearly gates,
For the beautiful soul an exit waits."
Then guarded ever so tenderly
In its flight thro' the untried ether sea,
It found its way from the heavenly clime
To an infant form in the Land of Time;
And the angel whispered, "Margaret — the Pearl,"
As fond hearts welcomed the baby girl.

The beautiful soul in stature grew,
In love of the holy, the pure, the true.
Tho' flattered by many the world called great,
Tho' tempted by riches, honor and state,
Simply and sweetly she took her way —
Loving and trusting from day to day;

Joining her voice with the praying band,
Helping the lost in the heathen land.

O beautiful soul, 'twas thy mission here
The mourner to comfort, the sad heart to cheer;
The Master to follow with willing feet
To the hovels where sickness and woe retreat;
The children to rescue from paths of sin,
And many a soul to thy Father win —
Not alone by thy words, or charity,
But the beautiful life that all could see.

Thou art gone, sweet soul, from our longing sight!
Thy place is vacant; and we to-night,
Think more of the sorrow thy loss has left,
Of the mourning hearts of those bereft;
Of the form thou didst dwell in — now pale and chill,
Yet dear, how dear! to our sad hearts still —
Than the joyful flight to thy native skies,
And thy welcome back into paradise.

O beautiful soul! O soul so white!
Thou'lt not forget, in thy home of light,
The friends of thy heart thou hast loved while
 here.
No! ever their spirits will seem more dear;
And, be it the will of the God above,
Thou'lt minister still of His peace and love,
And, come they early, or come they late,
Wilt welcome them each at the Pearly Gate.
(In affectionate remembrance of Mrs. C. J. McClung.)

THE MAGDALEN.

THE curtains are raised. At the window stands
A beautiful lady. Upon her hands,
And twined in her dark hair, many a gem,
As lustrous as those in a diadem.
She smiles on the cherub, her child, who now
Places a wreath of flowers on her brow.

How lovely the picture! while music sweet
Comes to the ears of the crowd on the street,
Who pass at the close of a winter's day.
Some smile, some wearily turn them away.
One stops and gazes, her soul in her eyes,
As viewing the beauties of Paradise.

Ah! but the contrast! the poor shrunken form
Shivers in rags. "Oh, how lovely and warm!
If I had but a crust! I'm *starving* to-night —
Hope! is there hope? everything looks so
   bright

Over there. Oh, Father in Heaven, forgive
A wandering penitent. Let her live."

She rings, then shudders,— the sound is so
    loud!
The door is opened. A menial proud
Advances, then looking with high disdain,
Takes hold of the door to close it again,
But pauses at hearing her anguished cry,
"The Lady! the lady! I starve — I die!"

A door is opened, out into the hall
Come the little child, and the lady tall.
The beautiful brow is drawn in a frown,
The beautiful eyes look scornfully down.
"Only a beggar! James, close fast the door,
How often I've told you "— She hears no
    more.

Out into the desolate, stormy street,
Braving the arrows of snow, and of sleet,
The bending form is now drifting along
Unnoticed amid life's hurrying throng.

For want, and woe, and care await
Many another at Poverty's gate.

What matters it now that once she was fair,
That fingers of love touched the golden hair;
That the half-clad feet, all numb as they roam,
Pressed the velvet pile in a happy home?
How clinging the arms of the mother fair,
Who rocked and sung to her tenderly there!

Drifting! Ah, yes! and, ere morning light,
The stars look down on a woful sight!
On the blue eyes, staring, and fixed, and dim —
On the wave-washed form. For the funeral
    hymn
Of the sighing wind, no more can she hear,
As she pulseless lies on her ocean bier.

O mother, with baby upon your knee,
What sorrows in future may hidden be!
In shielding your own, be pitiful, too,
To the many sorrowful ones, whom you

May find in the paths of sin and of wo,
And succor the tempted ere downward they
    go.

Fair lady in satin and costly lace,
You welcome each comer with queenly grace;
You smile on this gay cavalier, who stands
Awaiting the slightest of your commands;
Yet you know no better in life is he,
Than the poor lost creature, you'd scorn to
    see!

Because 'tis a woman, shrinking and weak,
With the blush of shame, or tear on her
    cheek,
O, turn not away! With anguish and fears,
Ready to bathe with her sorrowful tears
The feet of the blessed Savior of men,
There's many a penitent Magdalen.

IN MEMORIAM.

CLOSED are the gentle eyes
That oft would shed the sympathizing tear.
The orphan's cry
Shall pain her list'ning ear
No more to hear.
Now quiet lie
The hands, so quick to do the Master's will,
And joyfully —
Pulseless and still!

Sweetly she sinks to rest
Within the Everlasting arms asleep;
While angels blest
Vigils round her keep.
The upper deep
Sparkles with gems
Invisible to our weak, mortal sight —
The diadems
Of saints in white.

Farewell, loved friend, farewell!
They wait for thee upon the other shore.
We cannot tell
How soon may life be o'er;
And we, no more
Trammeled by clay,
Ethereal to the Throne of Love shall rise,
And meet, we may,
Beyond the skies.

·

Past is the Vale of Tears
To thee, partaker of the Savior's rest;
No doubt, no fear
Shall be e'en transient guest
Within thy breast.
As disappear
The shores of Time beyond thy waning sight,
To thee *how near*
Heaven's glorious light!

LAKE CHAUTAUQUA.

OH Lake Chautauqua! beautiful Lake!
   Hallowed, and sweet, and loved of the sun,
Here by thy lilied marge we'll take
   Rest when the long year's work is done.
      In our tiny boat
      On thy waves we float,
And the hours glide softly one by one.

Kissed by the zephyr thy shim'ring waves
   Dance into foam, and laugh on the shore;
Or when the tempest in anger raves
   Awake to echo its sullen roar,
      While softly we rest
      Like a bird in its nest,
Safe in the shade of the forest hoar.

Like a smile on the face of Nature — lo!
   Thou greet'st us afresh on each sunny morn;

And yet in the light of the sunset glow
   New gems of beauty thy form adorn.
      From this spot, remote
      From the world, we note
   Afar the weary and travel worn.

Thy classic shades! they wake again
   To the words of the noble who've won their place,
Arousing the nation by tongue, and pen,
   To thoughts of wisdom, to deeds of grace.
      So the soul may rest
      With no care oppressed,
   And yet expand into golden space.

Oh Lake Chautauqua! beautiful Lake!
   May our lives be as pure as thy waves, that we
The beauties of Earth and Heaven may take
   And mirror them forth as they're seen in thee!
      And with faith and love,
      From the Light above,
   A blessing and joy unto others be.

NIGHT.

The night is here!
I feel its shadows falling,
Wrapping me round in many a fleecy fold.
How shrill and clear
The whip-poor-will's loud calling!
The night-hawk by the darkness rendered bold,
Winging his flight in many an airy round,
Touches the ground,
Then darts away into the abyss of heaven!
A sheep bleats gently in its sheltering fold,
Calling the lamb that from her side has strayed.
Within the glade

The kine crop off the scented clover blooms,
Or sink with gentle low to dewy slumber.
  In countless number
The stars shine out upon the brow of even;
  While sweet perfumes,
Rich as of Araby the Blest, now hold
Our senses in sweet, rapturous thought enrolled!

IN THE TWILIGHT.

SITTING alone in the twilight,
  Watching the shadows fall,
    And the fading away
    Of the silver gray
  Into a sombre pall.

Fluttering leaves of Autumn
  Sigh and rustle around,
    And the song of the breeze
    Through the fading trees
  Has but a wintry sound.

Sighs from my heart are arising,
  Mists make my vision dim,
    For my thoughts travel back
    O'er a well-worn track
  As I hear the Evening Hymn.

IN THE TWILIGHT.

Slowly approaches a footstep —
 How firm and manly the tread!
  'Tis the one more dear,
  From year to year
 Since the time when we were wed.

Clasping a hand that has striven
 To lighten my every care,
  I sit and wait
  At the entrance gate
 Into the great Somewhere.

We sit alone in the twilight,
 For the day of life has fled,
  And the silver light
  Of the coming night
 Shines on my darling's head.

Oh, soon shall follow the morning!
 The night of winter be past,
  And the birds shall sing
  In eternal spring,
 Nor the sky be overcast.

MOVED TO TOWN.

Why, howdy! — how's the folks all?
  Did any of 'em come down?
Hain't seed ye fer a coon's age —
  Sense we moved into town.

Oh, yes, — we're fixed up pow'ful
  To w'at we wonct could be,
But a body's used to it d'rec'ly
  An' it's all the same, you see.

It's all the gals, — an' Marthy's,
  An' they set a mighty store
By the fandangles an' fixin's, —
  They're well enough to be shore,

But there hain't much comfort livin'
  (This world's a fleetin' show!)
I'd d'ruther be back a farmin',
  But they — well — they wouldn't go!

A body cain't have their druthers! —
　　How be I? pow'ful weak
Sometimes! — I guess it's rheumatics —
　　Hed 'em more'n a week.

I give my gals a schoolin',—
　　Their Mar had 'em Frenchified,
An' all done up in a jiffy —
　　I couldn't — if I'd a died!

Enj'y? — well — fer enj'yin'! —
　　There's many a thing to see.
The days out home passed so sudden,
　　Now — they're awful long to me.

There's a plenty o' time fer runnin',
　　If a body cared to go;
An' money — it hain't no objec'
　　Sence we found the coal ye know.

There's a heft of fellers comin'
　　To see the gals of a night,
But, I tell you — I don't much like 'em
　　They don't look overly bright;

They lisp an' hev an eye-glass —
  Well, they're good enough to me,
But they'd talk me blind direc'ly —
  They hain't my kind you see.

My wife? she hain't come down yit —
  She 'tended a ball las' night.
Her narves is kinder upsot,
  An' her head ain't mostly right.

The gals? oh, they're a restin' —
  It ain't quite twelve, you see,
An' that's their time fer breakfas' —
  Tho' it hain't the hour fer me!

I'm right smart riz o' fifty,
  An' I don't make no pretence
O' keepin' up with the youngsters,
  But I hope I've got some sense.

You wouldn't think it to hear 'em
  A tellin' me w'at to say,
An' how to set — till me hands, Sir,
  A kinder gits in me way!

An' me feet's too big to please 'em
  So these here boots is too small,
An' if there don't come a change soon,
  I'll not git around at all!

I feel a kinder okkerd —
  I *knowed* I would fer a bit,
These store clo'es 's *heaps* o' bother,
  Tho' *they* say they be a fit.

An' that's the way with the livin'—
  Tho' I s'pose 't'll come all right.
The sitiwation's, seemin'ly,
  Fer me a *leetle too tight.*

Goin'? I'm *glad* to 'a' seed ye! —
  You're home-some like an' kind,—
It hopes a person 'casional like
  To open an' air his mind.

Only a Glass.

"Only a glass!" The crystal cup,
Held by the jeweled fingers up;
The sparkling wine, in drops of light,
Vied with the eyes of beauty bright,
And sweet lips, wreathed in 'witching smile,
Parted with merry words of guile.

"Only a glass, why linger so?"
Only eternity can know
How strove a heart 'twixt good and ill;
The eye of love, the strength of will,
Only a moment,— then 'twas o'er;
He took the cup — he asked for more.

From day to day he downward sped,
Alas! he others downward led,
For evil will not dwell alone.
Too late the loved one would atone;

ONLY A GLASS.

She might prevent, she cannot save —
He sleeps within a drunkard's grave.

"Only a glass," the father takes;
With wine, or stronger liquid, slakes
The thirst of years. His little child,
With silken curls, and features mild,
Raises to him her rosy lip,
And begs: "Oh, papa, just one sip."

"Only a glass," the young man, too,
Must have with father, as he grew.
Wild youths he bids,— he drinks, he plays,
He wanders in sin's darksome ways;
Then half returns,— a gentle wife
Prays him to lead a nobler life.

Temptation is the lot of all,
He'd oft repent, as often fall;
For, weak by nature, how could he
Have strength to battle and be free?
Too late, alas! her hope how vain,
The poison to his fevered brain

Leaps up! To strike his babe he tries;
His mother forth to save it flies!—
One sudden blow, and all is o'er—
One life the less, one murder more!

In felon's cell he broods alone;
Remorse has claimed him for her own.

NORA.

By sad Appomattox river
Sadly, softly weeps a maiden,—
Weeps a maiden for the lost one,
Who has crossed unto the city,
City of departed brave ones,
Who have done their duty, nobly,
Done their duty, and are heroes
  Sadly moaning, weeping ever,
By the river ever flowing,—
Ever flowing to the ocean,—
Sits the lonely, hapless maiden
Who, 'twould seem, will mourn forever.
  "Oh!" she sighs, "he comes not to me,
Comes not to me, though I'm longing,
Ever longing to behold him.
He is sleeping by the river,
He, my brave, my noble hero!

Sweetly sleeping by the river.
I will wait until he wakens,—
Wakes to find his constant Nora
Ever loving, ever faithful,
Watching ever for *his* coming
That will make her sad heart happy.
Wake, my love, sweet eve's approaching,
Eve with all her holy beauties,—
All her starry eyes so brilliant,
Like the eyes of the good angels."

Softly, sadly moans the river,
But the night-hawk and the owlet
Shriek in discord wild above her,
Wild above her form a circle.
Circling through the air they watch her,
Watch her with their eyes so evil,
With their eyes so wild and cruel,
Watch her ev'ry gentle motion,
Watch her as she weeps for Melvin,
Weeps for him who always loved her.

Once again she cries for Melvin,
Cries for Melvin ever loving,
Ever true, and ever faithful

To the heart that's his forever.
And the night winds sigh for Nora.
And the wild birds cease their clamor,
Cease their clamor so unholy,
So disturbing and unholy,—
Fly away on abject pinion
Far away into the forest,
To the forest dark and lonely.

   Now a mist seems slow descending,
Slow descending from the Heavens,
From the Heavens towards the river,
Towards the river, darkly gliding
By the heroes' graves, where Nora
Waits and watches for her Melvin,—
Watches hopeful still for Melvin.

   Now the form seems close beside her,
Close beside the fearless maiden
Who would speak with the departed.
But with awe she now is trembling,
Trembling,— for 'tis Melvin's spirit,
Melvin's spirit that approaches,
That has heard her words of sorrow
Words of sorrow, and of pleading,

That once more he would be with her,
That she might once more behold him,
Might behold him, for she never
Could forget that fondly loved one
Who had made her life so happy.

 Now, indeed, he stands before her,
Stands before her as she gazes
At the darkly flowing river;
And he speaks in words so tender,
That her soul's subdued within her,
And a holy smile is playing
Playing o'er her lovely features,
Features now so calm, and placid.

 "Dearest Nora," says the spirit,
"Why so sadly art thou weeping,
Weeping by this lonely river?
Know'st thou not how short our parting?
Know'st thou not that soon in heaven, —
Heaven where we shall be most happy, —
We shall meet and dwell together?
Dwell forever true and loving,
Ever loving, pure and holy,
If thou truly love our Savior, —

Love and serve our gracious Savior.
He, — Our Father, — bade me hasten
To thy side, that I might comfort,
Comfort thee, and bid thee ever
Love, and serve, and praise Him truly,
Who has Heaven prepared, so holy,
For redeemed and ransomed spirits,
Spirits washed by Christ the Savior."
Lowly bowed the maiden, humbly
Crossed her hands upon her bosom,
Crossed her hands, and knelt so gently,
Praying that the Lord might give her
Strength to do what should be holy.

  Then the spirit of brave Melvin,
Melvin, who had done his duty —
Done his duty to his Savior,
Done his duty to his Country, —
Smiled, and said, ere he departed,
He departed for the mansion
Fitted up for him in Glory;
"Tell my father, and my sister,
I am happy, for my Savior
Washed my garments pure, and snowy,

In his blood, so holy, cleansed them,
And now all my sufferings over,
I shall live for aye in Heaven. —
Live in Heaven with my dear mother, —
She who ever led me kindly,
She who ever loved me fondly;
And with others she has cherished
I shall dwell; but bid them ever
Think of those who've gone before them,
And who soon expect to meet them, —
Meet them at the Gates of Heaven,
Meet them at the Throne of Glory."

Few more words he spake to Nora,
Bidding her prepare to meet him
In the Christian's fair Elysium;
Then he left her strong in spirit,
Left her high in her endeavor,
To submit and serve the Savior,
Serve the Savior who had given
Happiness to her loved Melvin,
Melvin now a ransomed spirit,
An inhabitant of Heaven.

And before her eyes he melted,

Melted thinly into ether,
As he rose on angel pinion,
Rose to greet his loving mother,
Who kept watch for him in Heaven,
Watched and waited though so happy.
  Nora rose. The dawn was breaking
Over the ever-flowing river,
And a light from Heaven was shining
In her soul so pure, and happy,
And she sang, in her rejoicing,
Sang the song of the departed
Who are evermore rejoicing,
In the bright celestial city.

Pat Doyle,

IN THE OLD EMIGRANT SHIP.

Oh, Docther — no — I'm no betther,
    Its worrse that I be the day —
But shure an' we all be's doyin
    From hiven an' the loight away.

It's Bridget that's d'i'd intoirely,
    An' me hearrt is loike to burrst!
An' the fayver wid fingers foiry
    Be'st burrnin' me mout' wid thurrst.

Ochone! me Biddy, acushla!
    I hear the sound o' the say, —
But look in the fut o' the berrth, sor,
    The babe seems quoit the day.

It cried last noight fur its mother,
    But doyin' she was, indade
The poor wake arrums cudn't howld it
    So jist be 'er soide it laid.

An' me Biddy — the tears was a rollin'
   From the eyes jist glazin' in dith,
An' the stiffinin' lips 'd quiver
   Betune ivery harrd drawn brith.

But thy say He's iver callin'—
   Owirra! wirra the day!
For there they'll birry me darlint
   A thousan' fathom they say! —

But bring the babe to its fayther
   Plaze, docther dear, if ye will —
O — howly Vargin — presarve it! —
   The darlint is could an' still!

Ye say it's now wid its mother?
   Yes, Docther,— on yes — I know —
But me hearrt kapes sich a batin'—
   Will — ye raise — me up? — jist so.

Why — Biddy? — I tho'cht ye'd lift me! —
   An' there the babe — on yer arrum —
An' mother! — what's this — the music?
   Back till the — ould home — home farrum.

LIFE'S CHANGEFUL DAY.

OUT in the morning air there rang
Quick axe-strokes, and the chopper sang;

Strong-limbed and stalwart, blithe and young,
Around his head the axe he swung,

Nor thought of being poor, half-clad,—
The joy of living made him glad.

The strokes have ceased. Ah! who doth pass!
A comely, dark-eyed country lass!

A blush, a smile, a furtive nod,
She trips away o'er leaf-strewn sod.

The chopper speaks with kindling eyes,
Then turns away, then looks, then sighs.

Then first he notes his out-worn clothes—
Love shows the shabbiness it loathes.

"Oh! ain't she han'some though!" quoth he,
"There's little show for th' likes o' me!

But all a man kin do I will,
And jest keep on a hoping still!"

He gave the log a mighty stroke,
That all the woodland echoes woke.

The maid half smiled, and turned again
And glanced adown the forest glen,

And "Ah, if he were rich!" sighed she,—
"But love mates ill with poverty!"

The sturdy arm, the spirit strong,
Have hastened Fortune's steps along,

A woodland, vine-embowered cot,
A garden rich, and pasture lot.—

What setting for a happy life,
Spent with a loving, thrifty wife!

So out a-wooing goes the swain
Nor finds his hopes and wishes vain.

For, soon returning, at his side
The dark eyed maiden comes,— his bride!

The years glide by with noiseless tread,
And glance on many a sunny head;
And little feet go pattering,
And children's voices laugh and sing.

Fair, smiling Plenty blessed the board,
And added to the little hoard
The farmer, careful, laid away
To serve when came life's "rainy day."
Their lives were full in sympathy
And loving care, and industry.

Once, only had they been estranged.
She deemed his love for her had changed
And secret grieved, but answered nought
When he her cause of sorrow sought.

Then slowly dragged the weary hours.
The world seemed full of faded flowers,
As day by day they grew apart,
With darkened brow, and aching heart.

Oh, what a fearful sight to see —
(To me a wondrous mystery!)
The sufferings of a little child —
So fair, so sweet, so undefiled;
Yet tortured on the rack of pain,
The hearts around it ache in vain,
With longings deep some ease to bring
By bearing all its suffering.

And when has fled the vital spark,
The mother's soul into the dark
Sits gazing. — Oh, to follow on,
And see the way her babe has gone!

From out the home three children passed
Within as many days. The last
Of their four darlings moaning lay
Within his cot. The waning day
Cast shadows on the pallid face
And seemed to add an angel grace.
And must *he* die? Together bent
The parents, and their sighs were blent,
And tears and prayers. Upon his breast
Again her aching head found rest,

While through its pain her heart was stirred
By fond caress and tender word.

And ever on through changing years,
Through trials, cares, through joy or tears —
Whatever might in life betide
They loving travelled side by side.

The child recovered; waxed, in strength,
Until — a man, resolved at length
To see the world, he wandered forth,
To travel round in South and North.
Then, hearing of the golden West,
He sought her mines in fevered quest.
At first he wrote. The years passed on

Still not enough of gold! Were gone
The Halcyon days of youthful light.
The Pleiad stars rose clear and bright.

What roused to life the dormant spark
Of love within his heart — so dark
O'ergrown by dull forgetfulness?
Sometimes a little thing will bless,

A smile, a word, a tiny flower
Hath o'er our lives a wondrous power.
The shimmering of a field of wheat,
Its golden lights, and shadows fleet,
The corn-flower's bloom, the swallows play,
May bring to mind some happier day;
And hearts will turn, 'mid love and tears,
To thoughts of home and childhood's years.

One night he sat within his camp
Alone. A feeble, flickering lamp
Made ghostly shadows on the wall.
He started as a feeble call,
A mournful wail — came to his ear.
Then shaking off the idle fear,
A moment bound him, turned about
And quickly reached the door. "No doubt
Some traveler who's gone astray.—
Ha!"—'twas a sound of sore dismay!

A woman lying in the snow —
Gasping and pale! a sudden flow
From parted lips — the crimson tide
Of life! — and so the woman died.

Still warmly to her boson pressed
They found, as in a sheltered nest,
A lovely babe, which through the storm
Had slept on cosily and warm.

The air was chill, the baby wept!
The heart within the strong man leapt!—
With tears he clasped her to his breast.

They laid the mother to her rest
Beneath the snow. This was the way
The miner found his waif and stray —
A little laughing, cooing dove
Which made him think of mother-love.

How fared the old man and his wife
As neared the Borderland of Life?
Much sickness, care and want had come
And changed the cheerful, pleasant home.
The old wife wept, the old man sighed,
But bravely strove their grief to hide;
And, when together, each would smile,
And cheerful speak in tender guile.

But lower bowed the stately head,
And slower grew the feeble tread.
The buzzing wheel, the cheerful song
That echoed when life's days were long
Had ceased, save as a crooning lay
Came faintly with the dying day;
For they were old and weak and poor —
Earth's hope seemed dead, and death was sure.

The night came down 'mid snow and sleet.
The wind blew cold. The aged feet
Close to the burning log — to warm —
Were placed. She sighed, "Ah what a storm."

The old man pressed her wrinkled hand,
"Dear wife — there is a Better Land."—

"Ay! Stephen, there's a promise sure,
We can't lose that, though we be poor!
And somehow, dear, it seems to-night —
I can't tell why — things looks more bright.
Our Robert — did I hear a knock?
Or was it the sound within the clock? —

I see it's warnin' now for eight."
Rap! rap! "Who can be out so late?"

"Come in!" A man with shaggy beard
Well bundled up in fur appeared,
Carrying in his arms a child.
Strange to be out a night so wild!

The old man looked in calm surprise.
The stranger turned with shining eyes —

"Mother" — she knew him! O, what joy!
"Father," she cried, "it is *our boy!*"

A sacred silence fell as hand
Clasped hand.
      "See! she can understand!"
Laughed Robert proudly, while the tears
Stood in his eyes. "Married? no fears!
Relation? no! one cold dark night
She came among the snow, all white,—
God sent my "Waif-and-stray" to bring
Me home to Mother."
      "Precious thing!

Welcome as any angel! dear,
Kiss Grandma!"

"Pap — you needn't fear
But what I've got enough for all."

The old man smiled, "Our wants is small."

"The sleigh out there is just chuck full
Of everything a'most. Now pull
This sleeve off if you can.— Come here!"
He called out at the door.

"Dear! dear!
Who have you left?" his mother cried,
"It's dreadful cold for those outside!"

"Only the driver — and a boy
That had no folks — here's Baby's toy,
Sit like a little lady there!—
You see I've got more than my share —
I've had a mighty sight of luck!
And this small chap's no end o'pluck,—
Well — short is — now he's mine. You see —
Jim! — here he is — 'he's just like me!'

You say? All right! you'll 'love him more?'
Well I shall not object. A store
I set by him already! There!
Mother — here, set it down! — *your* chair,
This is, as easy as shall be
Your life henceforth!"

"Dear me! dear me!
It *is* delightful! — Father, — you "—
"Oh, here's a seat to ease him too —
All stuffed and warm. Bring in the rest —
No — here! — sit down, and warm! that's best, —
I'll get the balance."

Then came store
Of all which they could need, — and more.

A happy evening! all so bright
Within the hearts and home. While white
The drifting snow upon the pane
Beat its cold fingers, all in vain, —
Happy foretelling of the days
Of peace and comfort. As the blaze

Shines brightly on the circle, we
May wish them all prosperity.
The old man murmurs "All these years,
God has been better than our fears."

AT THE GATES.

"SWEET saint with folded hands and brow serene,
  Waiting the white-winged messenger of rest,
With eyes full fixed on Heaven, e'en when the keen,
  And cruel darts of pain transfix thy breast,
Whence cometh to thy heart this peace so blest?
Upon the tender love thy soul must lean
Of Him whose will is always for the best,—
  Some of whose mysteries thine eyes have seen.
O precious saint, the Heaven and Earth so blending,
We fear thy days of ministry are ending!"

"And why," she said, "why wish to linger now —
But tarrying in the arms of cruel pain?
I would not murmur — no! I could but bow,
Did God so will the suff'ring o'er again.
But, could I fold my hands and hear the strain
Of angels, who should quick my soul endow
With immortality, — how sweet the gain!"
(We wiped the moisture from her dying brow.)
"There are no clouds," she smiled, our hearts divining;
"Upon the way the sun is brightly shining."

"O friend belov'd, would that on *my* face
The peace were written which I see on thine!"
Softly she murmured, "This is dying grace
Given at time of need by Power Divine.
You do not need it yet." The blue eyes shine

In loving tenderness. "When in my place
Just changing worlds — Your peace shall flow
   as mine."
I cried, "But if I weary in the race!"
"There is a cord," in sweet and solemn
   chiding,
"Doth bind the heart to Him in love abiding.

"How gracious God hath been! I prayed
   to live
To rear my little children. Day by day
I sought His presence — that He would for-
   give,
If haply they'd thought evil by the way.
And when beside my knee they knelt to pray,
When night had closed us in, we'd oft re-
   ceive
A sweet and blest assurance. So, alway,
Loving and loved, each year came a re-
   prieve —
Scarce should I call it so! — till at the ending
No babe shall weep — you've seen them o'er
   me bending.

AT THE GATES.

"I long — I long to go! — a month or two —
  What difference to them? but — oh! to me
Welcome release from weary hours, not few,
  Spent in the speechless throes of agony!
Time with its healing hand will set them free
  From sorrow's thrall— their spirits will renew —
Such is the way of life! And we shall be
All re-united soon.— The pleasant hue
Of all things round me — seems — so dull and fading!
Ah! is this death? then, welcome to the shading.

"So many on that side! more than I leave —
  With *such a welcome* there awaiting me!
As I shall look for you. How could one grieve
  To take the step into Eternity?
Better — far better! — oh, I hope to see
  Your faces *there!* — You all — you all believe?"

She slumbered for a moment, brokenly,
  "How sweet the name of Jesus! we must give
The praise of all to Him! within His keeping
Our souls abide, nor know of pain nor weeping.

"All, all is peace! for years it hath been so.
  I have no fear of — death? — mistaken word!
We but pass o'er the River, murmuring low,
  Into that Land where joyous song is heard.
I hear it in the distance — like a bird
  Singing of Spring ere yet the Winter's snow
Hath disappeared! the creature's heart is stirred
  By premonitions of the summer glow,
And waking of sweet Nature, from her dreaming,
To glorious loveliness of sunlight gleaming.

AT THE GATES.

"A picture faint of Heaven!" Then seemingly
  She floated 'twixt the realms of Life and Death.
Fragments of tender thought came dreamily
  As from a child half-wakened, and the breath
Came fluttering forth, as wild bird hovereth
  A moment still, then struggles to be free.
Calmly and peacefully she entereth
  Within the gates of Love and Mystery.
My aching heart beats heavily — a-weeping —
Counting its tears of blood as she lies sleeping.

But —"Peace!" for surely here the angels are,
  Though to our sight their presence is unknown;
For she on ent'ring left the gates ajar
  One little moment, and the glory shone

Within my saddened heart, while from the throne
Came sound of voices, singing from afar,
In harmony no words can speak. Alone
The music warms my soul, no night can mar
The visions blissful that a joy is making
This happy dream of life.— And then — the waking!

EPAMINONDAS.

I.

In this small effort quite without pretention
I will, as preface, casually make mention
That, if the pen fulfill the mind's intention,
There shall not be a pound of pure invention
To every ounce of fact; although extension
Be so desirable that intervention
To loose the bonds of weary soul retention
May, in a moment, spite of all prevention,
To clouds of fancy make a grand ascension,
Until, perhaps, it suddenly condense on
Some glacial fact, beyond its comprehension,
And in a thousand airy nothings fall —
Well — I believe for preface that is all.

There was a nation — so I've heard it said
By people who some ancient books have
    read —

Descended from the gods of olden time,
Whose deeds were mighty, and their lives sublime.
These were the heroes famed in olden story
Who victors lived, or died in martial glory.

I hardly think these ancient men so great
Were close related to the monkey state —
Like Father Adam,— who an ape had been (?) —
Poor man! he greatly suffered for the sin
Of being for an apple over-greedy —
Lacking in knowledge, tho' he were, and needy.—

But we'll not moralize. The fact remains,—
Those ancient people had their share of brains.
Their arts of warfare, and of stern defense,
Were no hap-hazard growth of vain pretense.
For noble minds, as noble deeds, the nation
Showed, by its plaudits, grand appreciation

We pass the age that glorious Homer sung,—
Blind Bard heroic! with the silver tongue;
Pass Codrus, good and brave, and many a
 name,
Like Solon! Pericles! of deathless fame.
Till jealous cities, leaving prey to others,
Fight to the death!— The bitterest foes
 are brothers.
Sparta and Athens thought themselves su-
 preme,
Thebes as a rival would not even deem.
With hasty anger set aside her claim
In the Great Council.—Scorned her honored
 name!
And fierce invective, only answer, thundered,
While deputies sat open-mouthed, and won-
 dered!

Who is this Theban, dignified and tall,
Martial and grand, yet kindly-faced, withal,
Toward whom as in a silence that is heard
The listening throngs bend down to catch
 each word.

Whose lightning eye around the circle
    flashes —
As it might burn their coward hearts to
    ashes?

Epaminondas! — whom Thebes made not
    great —
Who was himself the pillar of the state.
Ready for her to live, for her to fall, —
His country was his wife, his child, his all!
Wisdom and learning modestly were blended
With justice, courage, patience which ne'er
    ended.

His voice alone among th' assembled throng
Rose clear and earnest 'gainst the impending
    wrong.
Vain was the effort thus to stem the tide —
Hopes, wishes, — men themselves were swept
    aside! —
As well oppose the waves the rocks which
    dash on
As King Agesilaus in a passion.

II.

Epaminondas sat within his tent,
His heart was sad, his eyes on earth were bent.
"O not for fame, nor good of Thebes alone,—
'Tis for all Greece! her freedom she must own.
I would that all the world were full of gladness,
No act of mine might bring a tear of sadness!

"But 'tis for Greece!— my Country, 'tis for Thee!
Away unmanly sorrow! I must be
Strong as the strongest, battling for the right.
O powers of Zeus! aid me with your might.
Nor let the thought of suffering and sorrow
Un-nerve my arm for duty on the morrow."

Epaminondas came of noble race
Who in the songs of Greece had owned a place.
One of the greatest of the troop, full-grown.
Which sprung from earth when dragon-teeth were sown.

And now the chief of Theban statesmen living
His life, himself, his all most gladly giving.

And so the Cadmeian hero went his way,
And many a city armed her for the fray;
The whole peninsula from state to state
The Thebans traversed until just too late,
They reached the very doors of ancient Sparta,
But found that they had almost caught a
    Tartar.

For warriors stood full-armed. Her sentries
    wait —
Though many of her host return too late —
And deeds of prowess wake the voice of
    praise
On either side. But when the waning day's
Last twilight fades the Spartan mothers' wail-
    ing
Rises toward heaven in anguish unavailing.

On many a battle-field he won renown
For wondrous strategy. The victor's crown

Sat lightly on his brow.— Not for himself
Valued he honors, fame, or golden pelf.
"My parents!" thought he, "how their eyes will brighten,
And weight of years, and care, this gold will lighten."

III.

Vicissitudes are part of life's great story,
To-day upon a pinnacle of glory —
To-morrow shunned, and by the crowd passed by,
Which yesterday enthusiastic cry
And fair oblation made. Is *he* depending
On praise so hardly earned, so quickly ending?

"He is too proud," they said, "in his estate,
What can we do to make him seem less great?
We cannot wound his body,— that would make
The people love him more, for pity's sake.
Degrade him in his rank, and lofty station.
What shall he *then* be in our lordly nation?"

Most cruel wound ere felt, is when the dart
By a hand, trusted, aimed is at the heart.
The very men who helped to make him great
Ready to bind him to a cruel fate!—
This noble mark for cruel envy's arrow—
Wounded by charges (like them) false and narrow.

"A public scavenger! he'll ne'er descend
To work so menial. This will be the end
Of his career! The public will not choose
To call him forward if he once refuse."
But this he did not!—vanished their illusion—
Nobly he wrought, and put them to confusion!

O great Epaminondas! happy he
Who imitates thy virtues, and like thee
In whatsoever station be his place
Can e'en the humblest labor give a grace!
Who from "the Gods" doth glorious gifts inherit,
Ennobles all things by his gracious spirit.

War's tocsin sounds again! in dire alarm
The smith deserts his forge, the herd his farm,
They gather in to swell the arming host,—
But who shall lead them? who deserves the
    most?
" None but Epaminondas!" voices blending
Ring to the heavens so brightly o'er them
    bending.

With noble kindliness, and modest mien,
Enters Epaminondas, while the sheen
Of brazen shields upflashing to the sun
An omen seems of victory begun.
No acts of retribution e'er decreeing
He marches forth.— The foemen soon are
    fleeing.

On Leuctra's field — the troops were weary
    then —
They wavered for a moment — all the men —
But, "One step forward!" came the word of
    cheer
The voice belovéd sounded on their ear.

They struggle onward! — shields on lances rattle —
The phalanx yields — and Thebes has won the battle!

Thy deeds more than thy words, most noble Greek,
Our admiration, and our love, bespeak.
Nor should we mourn that ere thy waning sun
Had lost its glory, its full course had run,
Thy mortal form should rest in peaceful slumber
Thy soul awake to join the immortal number.

Thou goest not as a stranger to the skies —
Innumerable hosts around thee rise.
Thy spirit than the bright ones not less fair
Breathes in Hesperides its native air!
Sad sounds of earth thy funeral dirge are knelling,
Songs of immortals are thy welcome swelling!

'O warrior beside the Theban wall
For us thy last great battle pray recall.
And let us, Gentle Shade, once more with thee
Live o'er the glowing past, when gallantly
The Flower of thy Great City warfare waging
Held Greece in check, and stilled a monarch's
    raging.

The heavy sword, clasped as within a vice,
The shield light-lying on his heart of ice,
Moved as a throe of pain had racked his frame.
Then spoke he as awaked by touch of flame,
With visor closed he sat, alone the gleaming
Of flashing eyes told that he was not dreaming.

> "A morning without shadow
>   Upon the sunlit sky,
> A murmur like the ocean
>   As our army hastened by,
>
> "The mountains and the valleys
>   In verdure brightly clad.
> The song of men and maidens
>   Made all the woodland glad.

"But instant on our coming,
　These sounds of peace afar
Fled, as the mists of morning,
　Before the voice of war.

"Ah! Greece had many a matron
　Would arm her youthful son,
Cheering him forth to battle
　And think it deed well done.

"Though still he came, and silent
　Returning on his shield,—
'A glorious death!' they deemed it
　To die upon the field!

"The sunbeams on our helmets,
　And on our army bright,
Reflected at each motion
　A brilliant wave of light.

"While o'er us lightly floated
　The snowy plumes like foam,
And minstrels softly chanted
　The songs which breathed of home.

"For what could rouse our valor
  As thoughts of those who kept
A vigil for our glory,
  And watched while others slept?

"Behold! another army
  Comes bravely into sight
Soon as the waves of sunrise
  Have washed away the night.

"Our Theban army halted,
  Their arms were stacked around,
While shields to earth fell lightly —
  As 'twas their camping-ground.

"The Spartans all, aweary,
  When they had seen afar
That we were camped, and resting,
  Quickly their helms unbar.

"And soon asleep, or feasting,
  They lie upon the ground, —
Forgetting all but revelry
  They hear no warning sound.

"Then silently we hasten
  (Our leader's strategy)
To seize them in their weakness —
  But this is not to be!

"They see! they rise! they battle!
  Their cries ring forth in air
And wondrous deeds of valor
  Are wrought by their despair.

●

"O ranks of Lacedæmon,
  Of Mantinea fine,
Epaminondas' footmen
  Have broken through your line!

"The heavy Theban Phalanx
  Of fifty spearmen deep
Move forward,— strong, o'erwhelming,
  And all before them sweep.

Shield against shield, the foemen,
  And spear opposed to spear,
Contend the ground by inches,—
  Our victory! — how dear!

"For Fate cried out against us,
  And this she wildly said,
Standing among the fallen
  The dying and the dead.

"'Pursue the flying Spartans,
  Take vengeance, one by one;
But know that all your laurels
  Ere setting of the sun,

"'Shall fading turn to cypress.
  Let fall the sword and shield —
The torch reversed is smould'ring
  Your leader life must yield.

"'Weep! city of the fortress!
  No more thy star shall rise
To shine upon thy banners
  And lead to victories!'

"'Where is Epaminondas? —
  The bravest of the brave!
Fallen? impossible?' they cry,
  'The gods his life will save!'

"As leaves within the forest,
　Which rustle — then are still,
So fell each warrior's weapon
　Lacking the master-will.

"Slowly, half-stunned, and heavy,
　Turning, in silent grief,
With hearts bowed-down, we gathered
　Around our dying chief.

"'Childless you die, dear Master!'
　A friend said, at his side. —
The chieftain smiled in answer,
　Then spoke, just ere he died.

"'No! no!' he uttered gladly,
　'Two daughters have I here, —
The victory at Leuctra,
　And this of Mantinea!'

"Then drawing out the weapon
　Which pierced his gallant heart,
He closer drew his mantle,
　And instant did depart.

"So fell Epaminondas!
  So ceased the Theban power!
None other stood as champion
  In this most woeful hour!"

The warriors, in silence, moved away.
Upon the ruins shone the moon's pale ray.
And things which had been were as things
  which are
The present gliding into realms afar.
Time and eternity together blended,
I heard — "Thy deeds shall live when Earth
  is ended!"

MY BROTHER'S GRAVE.

NEAR India's shore is a beautiful isle,
   Kissed by the waves of Araby's sea,
Where the tropic flow'rs 'neath the sun's warm smile
   Open in beauty rare to see.

Oft to that isle does my heart return
   With a longing pain that I there might be:
By a little grave I sorrowing learn
   A lesson of mortality.

A lovely cherub, joyous and fair,
   Smiled in a circle of happiness.
But, alas! 'twas all too pure, and too rare,
   The hearts so loving long to bless.

MY BROTHER'S GRAVE.

Where the orange blooms, and the Palm trees wave,
   And the rose and myrtle in beauty smile,
Many tears were shed o'er a little grave —
   He sleeps in Ceylon's sunny isle.
Oh, oft in thought do I visit the spot
   On spirit pinions light as air,
While the waves moan softly, and weary not,
   As in song I dwell in those regions fair.

And as ever the perfumed breezes wave
   The boughs of the lofty old palm tree,
The orange blooms fall, like tears, on the grave
   Where my brother sleeps by the murm'ring sea.

THE SHEPHERD.

TENDERLY he leadeth,
  Day by day
His flock which feedeth
  Upon the heavenly mountains;
And o'er the sides of fair Libanus stray,
  Drinking from sparkling fountains.
And he doth seek
  With pains and care
The wandering, lest he lose them;
  The young and weak
He carrieth in his bosom —
  How safe their refuge, there!
  Sweetly they rest
  Aweary from their play
  Upon His loving breast
Our shepherd careth for his loved, alway.

MOTHERLESS.

Poor little nestlings!
The once warm heart is cold —
The mother-heart which ever throbbed for you,
With love unfailing which would ne'er grow,
  Love which could never have grown frail or old.
  Unlike the things of Earth
  Being of Heavenly birth
Would always have retained its roseate hue
  Brighter than gold;
  Gone the protecting wings
Ready to shield, to comfort, and to bless;
  The voice of hope and cheer,
    First on the waking ear —
Each lively note vibrant with tenderness!
  And eyes so clear and bright
Reflecting forth a spirit brave and true

From out their gentle light.
Love waked and ever new,
　　Passed into starless night.
　　And is this all for you?
　　Nay! for an angel sings
There is a fair Land, and a golden day,
Where those who love may dwell in peace
　　alway
　　And rest their weary wings,
　　　　　Dear little nestlings.

No Light Without a Shadow.

There's no light without a shadow,
   But we know the light is there.
There's no word of cruel import,
   But is follewed by a prayer.

All the sky may be o'er-clouded,
   But the sun is there the while;
Quickly is the tear of sorrow
   Followed by a happy smile.

Rushing tempests, pouring torrents,
   Wind-storms lashing up the seas,
Soon are followed by the starlight,
   And the scented evening breeze.

Then the face of Mother Nature,
   After all her wrath so wild,
Looks compassionate and loving
   On her frightened, wayward child.

Rest we then, although the darkness
   All encompassing may seem
We shall see a golden sunrise
   After life's sad, fitful dream.

MARA.

A RADIANT morn of love and light,
   A joyous company,
Sailing along on the waves so bright,
   While the winds blow fair and free.

A gallant bark in the noontide hour
   Asleep on the ocean's breast.
A tiny boat with the breeze so fleet
   Skimming from crest to crest.

A broken sky — a dashing sea,
   A boat with a rending sail!
   *   *   *   *   *   *   *
Only a sea-gull fearlessly
   Braving the ocean gale.

A broken life — a shattered love,
 Clouds whence the sunbeams fled
No rift to tell of the light above,
 For my sweetest hope lies dead.

The stars shine out, and the waves roll on,
 And the sailors upon life's sea,
Read not on my face that my heart is gone,
 And can never come back to me.

LEAVES FROM A LIFE.

THE evening is cold and misty. I'm sure I've worked with a will;
Yet here, in the gathering darkness, I'm sewing, and sewing still.
Well, now, I must light the candle; how numb my fingers are!
Shine on in your happy brightness, oh beautiful evening star!

And here in this little chamber, in an attic near the sky,
I wonder how they are living — the crowd who are passing by.
Indeed I should be lonely if you did not shine so bright;
Sweet star! my only companion, on this, my birthday night!

A year ago — but my fingers, — why should
    they tremble so?
Ah — there's a tear! how provoking! — on this
    beautiful vest! I know
Each spot will take from my earnings, — and
    now I can scarce get bread,
And this little rough sky-parlor as a shelter
    for my head.

I've often heard that there's nothing so bad
    but it might be worse,
How well I remember! 'twas quoted, some-
    times, by our good old nurse,
When some childish trouble came darkly to
    shut the sunshine away —

How different now seem those trials, in this
    later hour of the day!
In the little hand-glass, near me, I look, —
    and what do I see?
Item ; light hair *he* called golden, — grey eyes
    gazing back at me,

Not merry, and bright, and careless, but gravely questioning, where
Shall a place be found for the friendless, and a refuge from despair?

But, there! what a piece of nonsense! to reckon one's features so!
If ever I was a beauty I'm far from it now, I know —

Papa, if you could see me working away tonight
Beside the old tallow-candle — my only excuse for light
You would not think 'twas your "Baby," who met you upon the stair
When you called her "lily blossom," or "Lady Estelle, the fair."
With cheeks growing pale and hollow, and straight nose, pinched and thin.
What matter? I'll do my duty, and trust I at last may win,

Win what? enough to exist on? or is there a hope still left
Of future bliss, and enjoyment, for this heart so sore bereft?
Ah, who doth care for my sighing at setting of the sun?
Or who will mourn at my dying when my last hour's work is done?

My life seems almost a failure, I cannot live by my pen,
"With thanks!"—'tis pleasant to hear it, but bread is the food of men.
There is that last little poem, lying up there on the shelf,
Poor little brain-child, neglected! it seems a part of myself —
But there it must rest! for never can I spend more of my time
In trying to sell it to those who will not pay for the rhyme.
Have I not struggled bravely? even to taking a book

To a dozen doors, but I never could put
    on the agents' look.
There are certain things that I cannot do —
    I really *cannot* do!
All labor seems over-crowded, — the ways
    one can earn are few
Compared to the many needy. So many
    would music teach,
That, except to the noted masters, few pupils
    are left for each.
And painting, the same, — and writing! *that*
    is the worst of all;
The higher your thoughts, and hopes are, the
    heavier seems your fall.

What really is mostly needed is the talisman
    of 'a name',
So there's a terrible struggle to reach the
    Temple of Fame.
I am not much over-crowded, up here just
    under the roof —
Nobody comes to see me — perhaps I have
    held aloof.

Every day I'm so busy, from dawn till the set of sun,
That I have no time to neighbor.— Probably every one
Has heart, and fingers, as busy, throughout the cells of this hive,
Driving away the wear-wolf,— trying to keep alive.

Twenty! can I believe it?— ah, well, the years seem long,
When I think of the weary hours since I sang my birthday song,
That lovely, and golden morning, that woke me at glad eighteen;
But sad enough was the evening!— as many which go between.
Dear father! alone, he wandered out into the darksome night!
Oh, Father, did we not love you enough that you took your flight?
Indeed, indeed but I loved you,— you never will know how well —

But I never believe you meant it, for circumstances tell,
Sometimes, a different story from what was really the truth,—
So — this was an accident surely, and never a deed of ruth,
I've thought it out, over . . . and over! — The pistol was in his hand —
But how he could willingly leave me I never could understand.
What if his fortunes *were* shattered? he always was true, and brave,
And would sacrifice his pleasure a fellow creature to save.

Even the animals round him were sure of a word or smile.—
Would he kill himself? — leave me in trouble? indeed, it was not his style!
I cannot I will not believe it! . . 'Twas well dear Mother had died,
And so could not feel the sorrow — the slights which would wound her pride.

For she was so sweet and tender, and could
    not have battled at all,
With misfortunes which quite o'erwhelmed
    me,— pushed me quite to the wall.

The worst, is to be forgotten, cared for by no
    one alive.
Only a burdened worker, toiling to death in
    the hive;
Not one, not one is left me of all so happy at
    home.
One, only, alive — dear Harry! afar o'er the
    ocean's foam.

And he knows nothing about it; for when his
    ship set sail,
We drank at a happy fountain, nor dreamed
    that its springs would fail.
And — and — oh, Arthur! you left me without
    a line or a word —
You may not have known what tenderness
    your love in my heart had stirred.

But well I know had the sorrow visited you,
    not me,
To have made your life seem brighter the
    sweetest of tasks would be.

But here you have cruelly left me alone to
    the world and fate —
There! the candle's out! and the darkness
    seems all disconsolate,
To wrap me close in my sorrow.— Are any so
    sad as I?
I will lay me down to my slumbers, and dream
    of the days gone by.

A clear November morning! outside, on the
    roofs, I see
Diamonds a duchess might envy, sparkling
    alone for me!
How weary our hearts, and laden, in the
    night-tide lone! but now
A rainbow of hope and promise seems to rest
    on the morning's brow.

I am nearer Heaven in this eyrie,— nearer the
    sunlit sky,—
My soul awakes to the music of an angel pass-
    ing by;
While from my lips once sealéd, there carols
    a happy song.
The birds alight at my window — wondering,
    bright-eyed throng!
Come, pick up these crumbs, my beauties!— a
    breakfast I do not need.
Down into the city I'll hasten, for the "early
    bird" hath speed.

Who opens the door?— Ah, Nannie! good
    morning! thank you for this;
I do love flowers so dearly!— here, let me give
    you a kiss.
Poor little Nan! all fluttered she hastens to
    close the door —
I wonder if any one ever kissed the poor
    child before!
Ah, here is mine ancient neighbor, on the
    landing outside my door —

Pale and weakly she seemeth!— Oft has she passed before,
But I fear that care and trouble have made me selfishly blind
To the faces of want about me — not wilfully unkind —
No wonder she answers me coolly — so often I've passed her by.
But — no! she turns again smiling.— Is that a tear in her eye?
Does simply a word of kindness, when one is weary, or sad,
Make the world brighter? then, surely, we each can make some heart glad.

Out on the noisy old highway, trampled by numerous feet,
Oh, how it tires one to think of it!— think of the hearts which beat
Hopeless, or anxious, or joyous; aching perhaps with desire
To conquer in life's cruel striving; perhaps with a Heavenly fire

Burning within on the altar, while the weary, weary hand
Is upholding a weaker brother, who knows not alone to stand.
Working, and thinking, and praying,— cursing, and dying! they all
Struggle along on the life-wave sweeping from gutter to wall.

The sunshine seems to have faded! I am part of the bustling throng
Pushing, and hustled, and anxious, threading my way along —
Poor little girl! she has fallen!—oh! stand aside if you please.
There! I will pick up your matches.— You really will buy all these?
Thank you, sir!— poor little mortal! money will dry up her tears.
Which way do you go, little Match-girl? our way's the same, it appears.
Now, why do you look so sadly? you smiled a moment ago —

'Tis strange how Happiness leaves us, while
    a lingering guest is Woe!
Your "mother is surely dying?" ah! that
    is dreadful indeed!
"Starving," you say, "in a cellar?"... Take
    this loaf, and homeward speed.
Away through this darksome alley, through
    passages low and small,
It is strange that human beings can even
    exist at all!
No wonder with pallid faces they slowly and
    sadly creep
From the brightness of fashion's highway,
    who dwell in these mazes deep.

Oh, yes! through it all I follow! what else
    could a person do?
There's a fellow-creature starving — in the
    midst of plenty, too.
So smothering dainty feeling, which shrinks
    from the tainted air;
Repressing the fear of danger, and thinking
    a little prayer,

I enter — a room you call it? from the door
 comes all the light
To distinguish day from darkness.— Oh, you,
 whose lives are so bright,
Would for a moment you'd enter this place
 which they call a home,
With its few loose boards for flooring.— No
 wonder so many roam —

Poor creatures! or take the jewels you prize
 for their children's bread.
Perhaps some may be forgiven, and you will
 suffer instead,
For withholding the good that's given you
 to minister unto them
Who stand in need of the blessing. No one
 could *I* condemn,
Who have lingered within the shadow of my
 own poor, darkened heart,
And absorbed in my sorrows, and fancies,
 have forgotten to do my part.
But the woman! in the twilight of the room
 I could scarcely see,

E'en when I was more accustomed.— Her
    large eyes fixing on me
She strives to utter a welcome.— No sound
    from the lips outcame
So parched with the wasting fever, destroying
    the famished frame.
But the mother-love is stronger than even
    the power of Death,
For her arms still clasp her children, though
    shorter the lab'ring breath.

And there they lie on her bosom when her
    face grows cold ; and still.
A policeman passing hastens to learn what
    may be my will,
And relieves me by giving orders to the neigh-
    bors who crowd around,
When they hear of the death of the woman.
    But where shall a home be found
For the little children wailing the death of
    their mother dear?
The poor-house? oh! let me ponder — what
    if these children here

Were mine! could I bear to leave them to the
    hands of a cruel fate —
To be scattered — bound as servants? Per-
    haps when it was too late
I might find these very children warped and
    forced into sin.
What can I do? — Poor babies! my garret
    shall take you in.

*   *   *   *   *   *

Night. As my busy fingers fashion from gar-
    ments old,
Clothes for three young children, sweetness
    there is untold
In the thoughts that sing in the shadow of
    mem'ry in my breast;
Softly they sing, like at dawning, the birdlings
    in their nest.

Strange how this seeming trial is a blessing
    in disguise,
A Special Providence sent me to 'lighten my
    blinded eyes.

And, surely, whatever happens, or whatever
　　I must endure,
I have learned a lesson I needed, and will
　　always be kind to the poor.
Charity blesses the giver more than the one
　　distressed,
And the heart that loves little children, by
　　God is specially blessed.

Surely these three little darlings, lying so
　　sweetly asleep,
Were sent,— for I did not seek them.— God
　　grant I may purely keep
And render Him back these jewels I wear for
　　a little while.

Ah, yes! sweet babes, in your slumbers well
　　may you sweetly smile,
For the angels are watching o'er you. Your
　　Father a charge has given,
And your slumbering forms are lying close at
　　the Gate of Heaven.

Nothing of worth came with them — only this
　　well-worn book ;
I will cease my sewing a little, and take a
　　casual look.

Perhaps it contains their ages, or thoughts
　　from the mother-heart
Now cold and still in the darkness. Alas!
　　what a meagre part
Had she — what! am I not dreaming? *His
name* — his familiar hand!
And who was this poor, sad woman? I can
　　not yet understand.

"From Arthur" — what next? 'tis blotted,
　　or half-defaced by tears.
Surely that word is "Sister." — This writing
　　below appears
As formed by a hand quite shaking, and weak,
　　for the letters run
One into the other. Poor "Susan!" she had
　　even then begun

To fear that the day was coming — how sad!
   when she all must leave.
No wonder the words so tremble! no one
   lives but would grieve
At thought of the little children — tho' her
   life was dark indeed
After her husband had left her — when all of
   their good with speed
Had been spent in his downward courses,
   from room to room they went;
Till at last the landlord had left them in this
   cellar, for lack of rent,
Taking their goods in payment. Ah, Susan!
   — had you not sent
To the father who once loved you? — your
   mother was dead, I know,
But the brother would have helped you, *this*
   I feel sure, although
To me he acted untruly. "I write, but no
   answers come.

"Oh, father, I've oft been sorry I ever left
   you, and home.

But, oh! as you hope forgiveness, have pity,
    I pray, on me,
And these little children weeping for food,
    around my knee.
You never knew what a coldness, a sinking
    there is of heart
As you feel the pangs of starvation. — Father,
    your tears would start
Did you see an animal suffer the woes which
    now are mine —
Seeing my little ones failing, — Saviour, some
    angel incline
To come ere these precious babies — I am
    too sad and weak
To even complete the sentence. — No word
    can I now speak."

Oh, to have known it sooner! what woe
    might she have been spared!
Poor dearest! more than sister! my last
    should you have shared.
Too late! all that remaineth is to do my
    duty in love

To the half-starved darlings — so precious —
    strange that she could not move
The heart of the stern old father, who, though
    he had cast her off,
At the thought of asking bounty of any one
    else would scoff!
The letters of course were " missing," — never
    by them received,
At even the *thought* of cruelty either of them
    would have grieved,
But now! again to my sewing! I must work
    as well as think,
Three little mouths will be open, needing
    their meat and drink.
Three little hearts to link me anew to the
    wheel of life —
Three little hearts to love me, to make my
    future so rife
Of tenderness, joy and blessing, that sorrow
    shall be forgot
And I shall render thanksgiving for the sweet-
    ness of my lot.

    *   *   *   *   *   *

Once more on the street. I hasten — taking my work to the store.
Surely they'll pay me this evening, — 'twill be two dollars, or more!

What shall I do with the money?... The children are playing now
Up in the little sky-parlor... I have to consider how,
As much as any old miser, to spend ev'ry precious cent.
How often in thoughtless childhood far more than that I have spent
On a single toy... Well — the children must have what they need to eat,
Some extra clothes they are wanting, and shoes for the busy feet.
Ah, we must "consider the lilies, which neither toil nor spin,"
For my hands seem all too feeble a goodly living to win.
But — was the mother less faithful? — she perished of want and care.

God help us, who are so needy! ... We're
    blessed with sunlight and air!
And poor little Paul and Jennie, the babies
    near three years old,
And motherly five-year Gretchen (ah, what a
    place they hold
In my heart) — how they laughed to see, and
    play in the sweet sunshine
Which dancing came through the window,
    under my ivy-vine.

The rough, and paintless rafters, to them were
    a beautiful sight,
For, here and there, through the shingles came
    a tiny pencil of light.
While pictures from *Harper's* and *Leslie*,
    pasted upon the wall,
Were things of wonder and beauty! so they've
    enjoyed it all,—
From the crackers, and dry bread toasted,
    soaked in water and milk,
To the chintz-covered lounge and rocker, — in
    their eyes finer than silk;

For bright are the leaves and roses, and soft to the little feet
Fresh-washed, and tender, treading back and forth on the cushioned seat.

Ah! here is the store! — I *dread* so to go to that surly clerk;
I *hope* he'll be in good humor, and not find fault with the work.
"Good-morning!" (he does not answer!) "the work which you gave, you see,
Is finished, — I hope, to your pleasure, — here 'tis" — (He gazes at me!)
What shall I say? — from the window I look out on to the street —
"Please pay what 'tis worth," I falter, unable his stare to meet.
Alas! he is praising "my beauty!" such compliments come but ill
From such lips and eyes! — Oh, my Father, from evil protect me still!
I tremble! — will he not pay me? . . . Insult! oh! how can I live!

There! I've spoken so that he's angry, and
  says he'll "never forgive!"
No pay! — my heart's in a ferment, as I
  hasten out into the street.—

Oh! whose are the hands that clasp me?
  whose are the eyes I meet?
As mine, all tearful and wretched, sudden and
  swift, arise
As a tone once sweet and familiar,— then
  change to a glad surprise.

Who but the one who loves me? who always
  has done the same
Through the months of a weary illness! who
  never has been to blame,
And though in a rising city far out in the
  distant West
Their family all are living, he still has kept
  up his quest.
And the sister who long had left them,— he
  had searched the city through
But feared he never should find her—(here I
  told her story too),

For though discouraged, and saddened, he faltered not in intent
Of finding "his own" he tells me,— and his princely head is bent
In loving and tender chiding,— as we sit a carriage within —
Going in state to my lodgings. Another life we begin.

NAN.

PART I.

Yes, sir! my name it's "Nan," sir,
  "Another name?"— hev you?
Why! what d'ye say? — I'm "answerin'
  One question by askin' two?"

You got two names? all right, sir,
  I guess I'm jest too poor.
Haint got no father and mother —
  You might 'a' knowed that, sure,

'Thout askin' — it's a bother! —
  What else d'ye want to know?
Oh, that lady they called "Steller"
  She moved out long ago.

"Up near the stars?" you'd think so!
  A-climbin' up them stairs —
But I guess she liked it, druther, —
  Better nor anywheres,

Till her feller he brought a kerridge —
  I tell you! wasn't it some!
You might 'a' thought they was goin'
  A-ridin' to Kingdom come!

An' the childern she'd got 'dopted
  Didn't they take a shine! —
Tell you I don't want nothin'
  Of that there kind in mine!

"Where d' I stay?" well, sometimes
  I stays most anywheres —
I *hev* slep' in a goods-box
  Like-wise under the stairs, —

But there's old Granny a-callin'
  'Most a-top o' the sky —
Yes, sir! I calls her Granny —
  Jest 'cause she ain't — good-by!

You'll "call again?" oh, don't trouble!
  I mostly isn't at home.
Yes! I really did "love 'Steller'"
  If you want to know, well come

Some time to the very top here,
  And Granny she'll talk you blind
On that there subjec' terec'ly —
  If she happens to feel inclined.

You'll come up now? — did I ever!
  Well, I'll jest run up an' see,
For Granny — she might turn rusty
  An' lay her finger on me.—

Law sakes! what a precious bother —
  A-havin' to go up stairs,
For that there dude in the entry —
  A-puttin' on all them airs.

Here, Granny! poor old Granny! —
  What did you want o' me?
Here — never you mind a-risin'—
  I'll bile up yer cup o' tea.

'T won't take me not but a minute,
   I ain't so awfully slow.
You're "tired?" well, I might a-know'd it
   I'll tell the gentleman so

As wanted to come and see you.
   You'd "ruther see him?" oh, well!
I'll go this terec'ly minute,—
   Tell you he's pretty swell!

Guess I don't care what *he* thinks—
   But I'll jest slick up my hair,
And wash my hands in yer basin—
   Granny—you wouldn't care?

Don't matter a pardigle no way
   But—will you give me a pin?—
Gethers is al'ays a bother—
   Hevin' to fasten 'em in.

Would you ruther I'd go leave ye
   To talk to the gent a bit?—
Here he comes!—yes, here's the room, sir.
   Ah—"Steller's?" this one's it.

All fixed so pretty with papers —
    Them pictur's round the wall;
An' that's her bed, an' her cheer, sir —
    I ain't "a-cryin'" at all! —

You'd cry, I guess, if she'd left you —
    The only friend as you had
What was tryin' to treat you good, sir,
    And learn you what wasn't bad. —

"Give me money?" you're jokin'!
    She hadn't any to give!
You can bet your last red cent, that she
    Had to keep scratchin' to live.

An' after them childern a-comin' —
    Didn't stay long, you know,
She looked so much like a' angel
    I was *that afeard* that she'd go.

They say that they 's awful happy,
    Somewhere — off where they went.
They give some money to Granny,
    But I guess that it's all been spent;

For she has to be close an' keerful —
 "What does it matter to me?"
Well, what a question! — I — like her
 Because she needs me, you see.

It's awful nice to be wanted
 An' not to be driv' away. —
"Would I like to hev a schoolin'
 An' hev to do nothin' but play?"

Ha! ha! what a pretty story!
 I'll take it to little "Stell."
"Who's she?" why, my little sister —
 Leastways I love her as well,

So I *guess* she is. She's a beauty!
 I tell you now for true. —
You "meant it really and truly?"
 Then I say goody for you!

Lemme see! — I'd be awful lonesome
 'Thout that sweet little face, —
But what's that matter? it's better
 To put little "Stell" in the place.

She jist was born for a lady.—
   Say, Mister, do as you say,
You may edicate little "Steller"—
   I named her that one day

When the pretty lady looked smilin',
   An' give me a pleasant word —
First from a real lady
   'At ever this child had heard.

"Her name before?" oh, no matter,
   Call her nothin' but that.—
Dunno what I'll put on her —
   Hasn't no bunnit nor hat.—

Oh, there's Granny a-callin!—
   S'pose she wants to see *you*.—
Say! *she* said that God would bless us
   As we to others might do.

You'll not forgit it, will you?—
   Be good to poor little "Stell!"
All right — why! be you "Harry,"
   Brother to *her*? do tell!

I — think — I'm feared,— I was sassy —
  Thought you was peekin' about
Like some o' them newspaper fellers
  Seein' what you could find out.

Here, Granny — it's only *her brother*,—
  There! he's in.— If I'd knowed it afore!
Her brother! good sakes! — I'd 'a' gladly
  Crep' out through a crack in the floor!

These rickety stairs — how they tremble —
  As I jump three steps at a time.—
Here's a stone and string — a knocker
  For the door of that cross Mis' Prime!

Won't she be mad? — I'm forgettin'! —
  Her baby it died last week.
It wouldn't be fun to plague her.—
  Oh, "Stell" — come listen me speak!

PART II.

Softly the morning sunlight
  Crept to a little bed,
Laying its fingers lightly
  On a sick child's restless head.

Sweetly she came from the shadow
    Of a troubled, anxious sleep,
As one at kiss of a mother
    Who doth watch o'er her darling keep.

The hospital nurse spoke gently,
    Pressing the little hand
That weakly wandered towards her,
    And tightened a snowy band

Over the sun-browned forehead,
    Over the curly hair;
Then opened the window softly
    To let in the morning air.

Patient, and uncomplaining,
    Though suffering all the while,—
Meeting each look of kindness
    With a wan but grateful smile;

Shattered, but sweet in dying,
    Through the waning hours she lay,
Like the bud of a sweet wild-rose tree
    That a storm had broken away.

In a room below were gathered
   A group whose eyes were dim,
As the doctor rehearsed a story—
   One of sadness to him,—

Of poor little Nan now lying
   Just at the Gates of Death.
"I was driving," he said, "through the city
   With horse almost out of breath—

So urgent the call—when hearing
   Close to his feet a cry,
I reined him up, but he stumbled!—
   Never until I die

Will the sight I saw be forgotten!...
   'Twas a *terrible* thing to me!
Oh—I cannot...well—we drew her
   From under the horse's knee,

And picked up the little fellow
   She had given her life to save,—
Some one's toddling baby
   Which had wandered out. The brave,

Glorious little creature! . . .
    I carried her quickly here.
But — well — you shall see her directly —
    Her hours are short, I fear.

One word, I'm not a believer
    In much that the parsons preach,
But I tell you she's *lived* a sermon
    Beyond any power of speech.

This way. There — I think she hears you.
    Good morning! — you're better alone.
Poor little feet — just crossing!"
    He murmured in tender tone.

"They have come!" the kind nurse whispered,
    "Do you not understand?"
As the dark eyes wandered wistful.—
    Estelle pressed her small brown hand.

"Ah, yes," she murmured, "dear lady!
    I've tried to do what you said,
But the words was hard to think of —
    Mebbe I've done 'em instead.

You said 'He's so kind'— He'll forgive me,
   Don't you reckon He will?
I never knowed nothin' about Him
   Till you tell'd me. I jist lie still"—

They are weeping who stand around her,
   Nor speak as the faint tones cease,
For softly o'er her is stealing
   The hand of eternal peace.

"Poor little Nan," sighed Harry,
   "I wish that you could be well!"
Gently she murmured —"'Member,"
   And nodded toward little "Stell,"

Then smiled — her hand in "the lady's,"
   As weeping, they knelt by her side,
"Think"— a quick breath —"Granny"—
   So Nan, the self-giving, died.

www.ingramcontent.com/pod-product-compliance
Lightning Source LLC
Chambersburg PA
CBHW021731220426
43662CB00008B/795